Table of Contents

Introduction

For more than 25 years, I have been conducting professional development sessions in mathematics for teachers, math coaches, and curriculum supervisors. At the beginning of these sessions, I often ask participants to list two or three major concerns they have regarding their work as math educators and leaders in their regions, districts, and schools. Over the years, I have collected, analyzed, and addressed thousands of these concerns, and it amazes me *that the concerns are always the same!* So much so, that it has become predictable which concepts, topics, and skills will appear on each new list. The following are a mere sampling of expressed concerns that are constants:

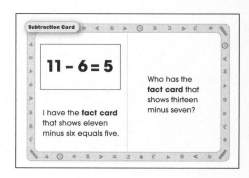

- *How can I teach the prescribed content and process strands at my grade level when my students are not ready for them?*

- *My students do not have mastery of their basic facts!*

- *Measurement skills are a major concern, especially in the area of metrics.*

- *Mathematical language necessary to communicate is often an area of need.*

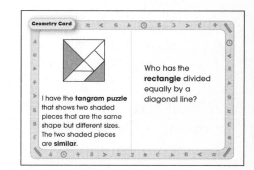

- *Problem-solving skills are not an integral component of a student's background, e.g., make a model, draw a picture, look for a pattern, make a simpler problem, guess and check, etc.*

The expressed concerns of math leaders and classroom teachers that I have collected over the years have led me to create activities designed to support foundation builders—early childhood and elementary-level classroom teachers—in their efforts to help their students master concepts and their related skills.

The activities in *Ask & Answer Interactive Math Practice* were not developed or intended to teach concepts related to addition, subtraction, measurement, and other mathematical skills. Rather, they were designed to serve as a means to *reinforce and strengthen* basic skills with automaticity and accuracy while promoting communication and developing mathematical language.

Several years ago, the National Reading Panel issued a report titled "Teaching Children to Read—An Evidence-Based Assessment of the Scientific Research on Reading and Its Implications for Reading Instruction." One of the key areas addressed in the study is *fluency*, which is "generally acknowledged as a critical component of skilled reading." (See National Reading Panel, 3–1.) While the parallel may not be direct, it is my hope that the activities in this book will promote and support a fluency in mathematics that leads students to acquire mastery of concepts and automaticity (speed) and accuracy with regard to their related skills.

How to Use This Book

Inside, you'll find six sets of *Ask & Answer Interactive Math Practice* cards—a set each for reviewing basic concepts in addition, subtraction, money, time, measurement, and geometry. Each set consists of 40 cards with two sides: the left side features the *Answer* part, while the right side is the *Ask* part. The first student (or you, the teacher) starts by reading aloud the left side of the first card, then asking the question on the right side. Students have to listen carefully and pay close attention to see whether the left side of their card contains the answer to the question being posed. If it does, the student with the matching card reads aloud the answer then asks the next question. This cycle of asking and answering continues until the last card is read.

To facilitate this interactive review, start by making two photocopies of each complete set of cards. Keep one set intact. This will be your script to help you keep track of the correct order of cards. Cut apart the other set, making sure that each card has both sides. Each student should have at least one card. Whenever possible, provide students with more than one card, but make sure that an individual student's cards are *not* in sequence, so that a student doesn't answer his or her own question. NOTE: To ensure that every student can participate successfully, you may want to review each card and distribute the cards to individual students based upon their level of mastery of a topic.

Encourage students to study their cards and anticipate what question might be asked that would fit the answer that they have. As students develop confidence, understanding, and mastery, they can be given more-challenging cards.

At the onset of the activity, students will recognize the need to be attentive if they are to hear their classmates ask, *"Who has…?"* As students gain understanding and confidence in the process involved in this activity, you may elect to have students respond in a more efficient manner, for example, not repeating what has been asked or simply stating the basic fact and its answer.

You may also want to make copies of several cards for display on an overhead projector. This will help students become familiar with the graphics, representations, and pictures that they might encounter in the texts and on state examinations. Representation is a key process strand found in the NCTM's *Principles and Standards for School Mathematics*. It promotes the use of representation to communicate mathematical ideas; translate representations to solve problems; and use representation to interpret physical, social, and mathematical phenomena. The challenges posed on the cards contain graphics (representations) that can be used to fulfill the key points found in the process strand.

You can also use the individual cards as the basis for writing activities. Invite students to write their own individual and/or small-group response to a card on their desk or one projected on a screen. Later, they can work cooperatively and collaboratively to create a series of topic-related questions that parallels the *Ask & Answer Interactive Math Practice* format.

— **Joseph A. Porzio**

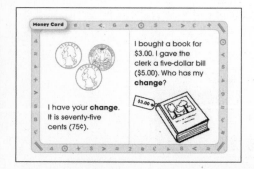

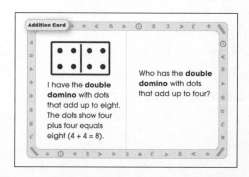

Connections to the NCTM Standards

Standard	Addition	Subtraction	Money	Time	Measurement	Geometry
Number and Operations	•	•	•	•	•	•
Algebra	•	•	•		•	•
Geometry					•	•
Measurement			•	•	•	•
Data Analysis and Probability				•	•	
Problem Solving	•	•	•	•	•	•
Reasoning and Proof			•	•	•	•
Communication	•	•	•	•	•	•
Connections	•	•	•	•	•	•
Representation	•	•	•	•	•	•

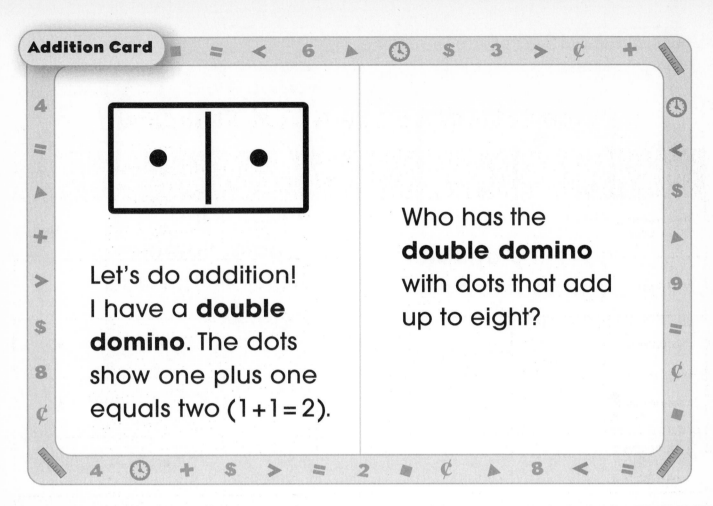

Let's do addition! I have a **double domino**. The dots show one plus one equals two (1+1=2).

Who has the **double domino** with dots that add up to eight?

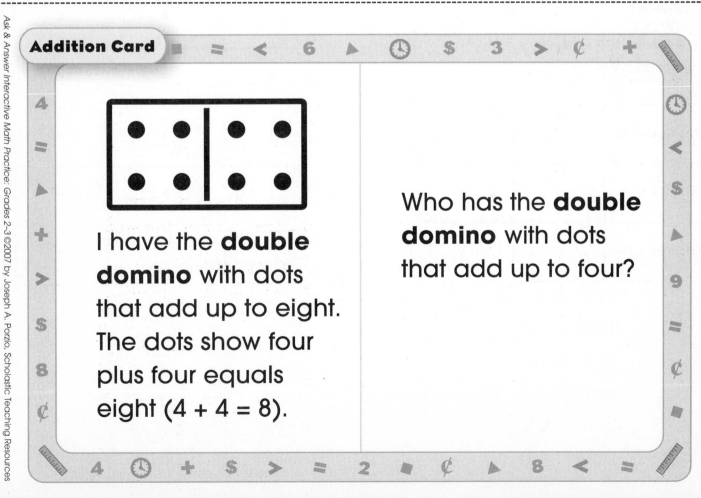

I have the **double domino** with dots that add up to eight. The dots show four plus four equals eight (4 + 4 = 8).

Who has the **double domino** with dots that add up to four?

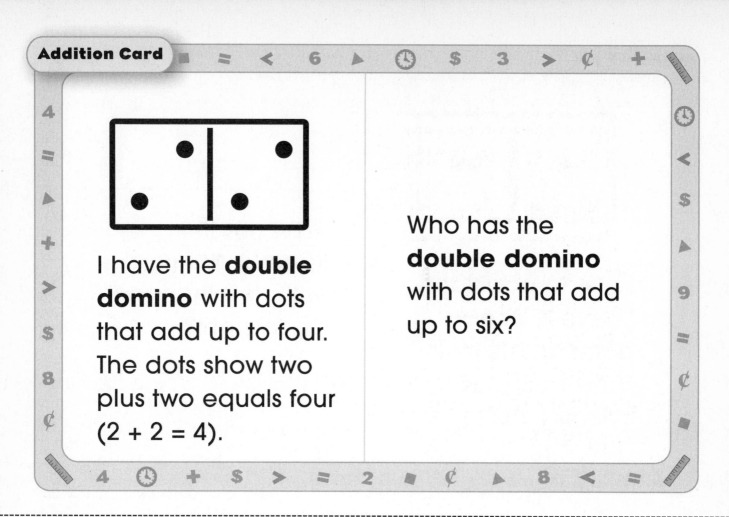

I have the **double domino** with dots that add up to four. The dots show two plus two equals four (2 + 2 = 4).

Who has the **double domino** with dots that add up to six?

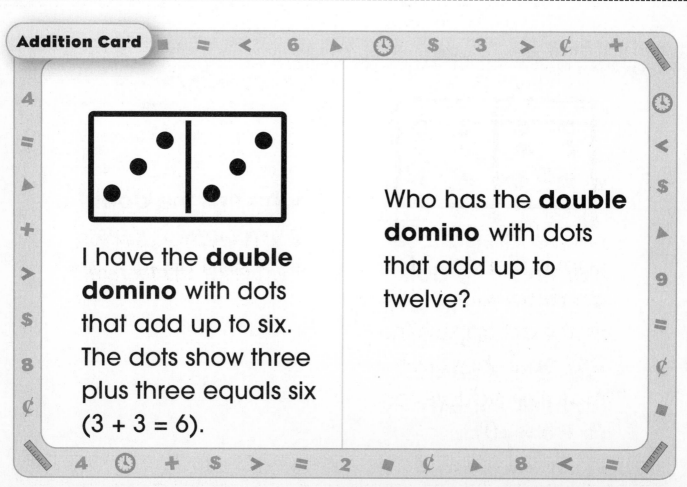

I have the **double domino** with dots that add up to six. The dots show three plus three equals six (3 + 3 = 6).

Who has the **double domino** with dots that add up to twelve?

Ask & Answer Interactive Math Practice: Grades 2–3 ©2007 by Joseph A. Porzio, Scholastic Teaching Resources

Addition Card

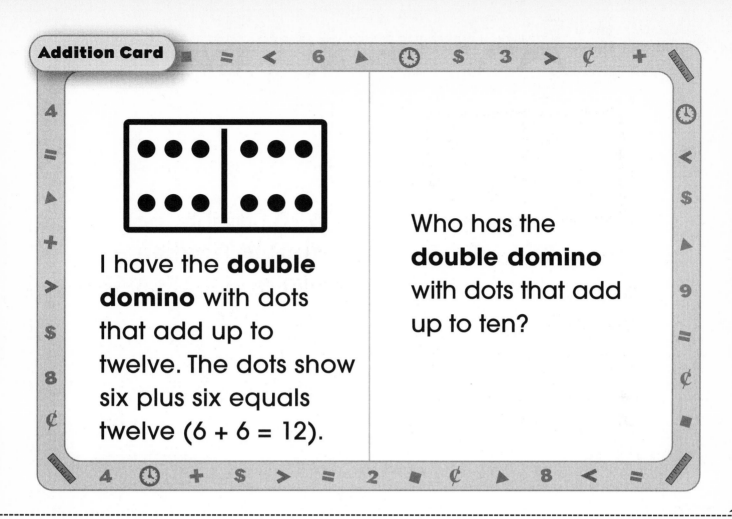

I have the **double domino** with dots that add up to twelve. The dots show six plus six equals twelve (6 + 6 = 12).

Who has the **double domino** with dots that add up to ten?

Addition Card

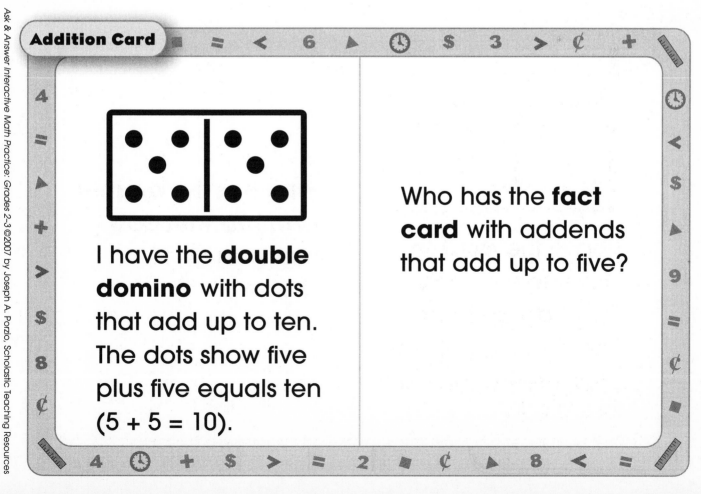

I have the **double domino** with dots that add up to ten. The dots show five plus five equals ten (5 + 5 = 10).

Who has the **fact card** with addends that add up to five?

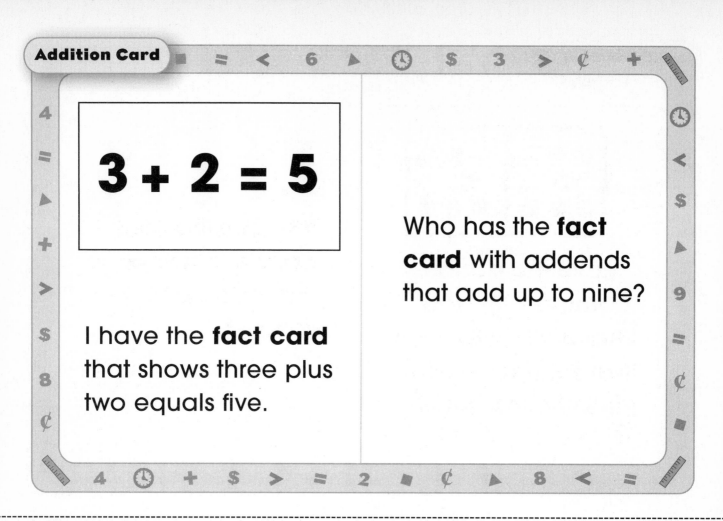

Addition Card

$$3 + 2 = 5$$

I have the **fact card** that shows three plus two equals five.

Who has the **fact card** with addends that add up to nine?

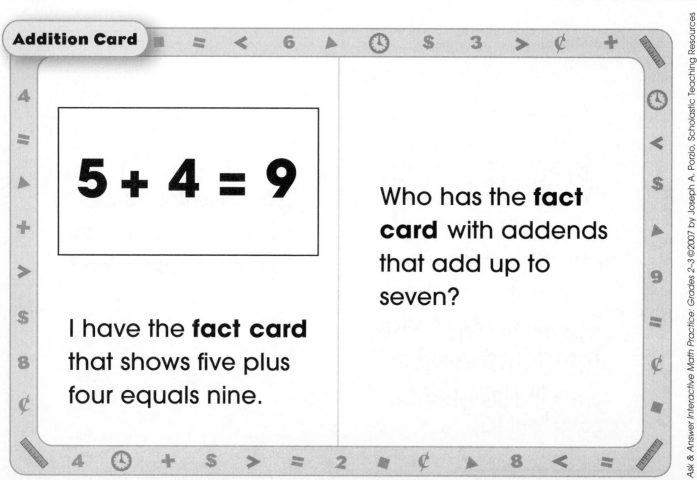

Addition Card

$$5 + 4 = 9$$

I have the **fact card** that shows five plus four equals nine.

Who has the **fact card** with addends that add up to seven?

Ask & Answer Interactive Math Practice: Grades 2–3 ©2007 by Joseph A. Porzio. Scholastic Teaching Resources

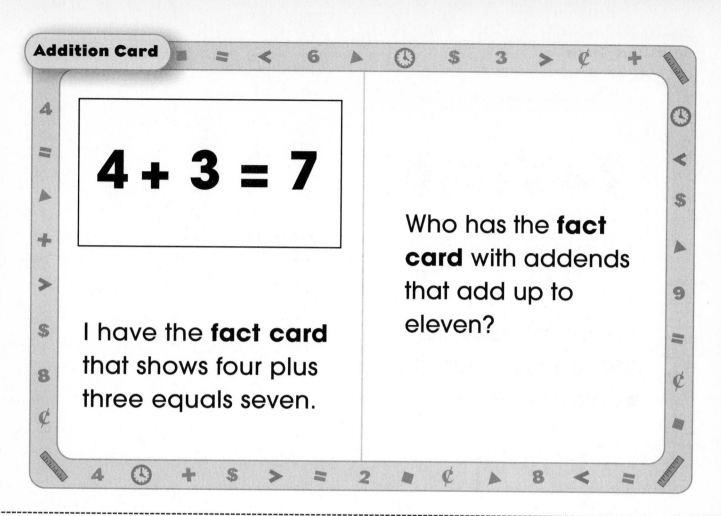

4 + 3 = 7

I have the **fact card** that shows four plus three equals seven.

Who has the **fact card** with addends that add up to eleven?

Addition Card

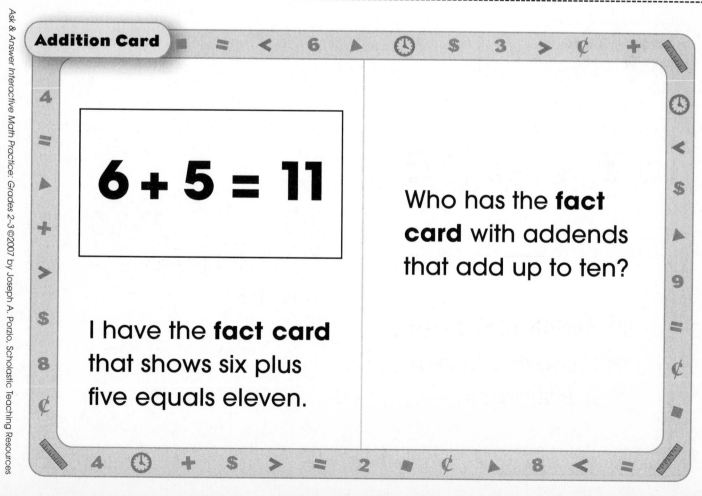

6 + 5 = 11

I have the **fact card** that shows six plus five equals eleven.

Who has the **fact card** with addends that add up to ten?

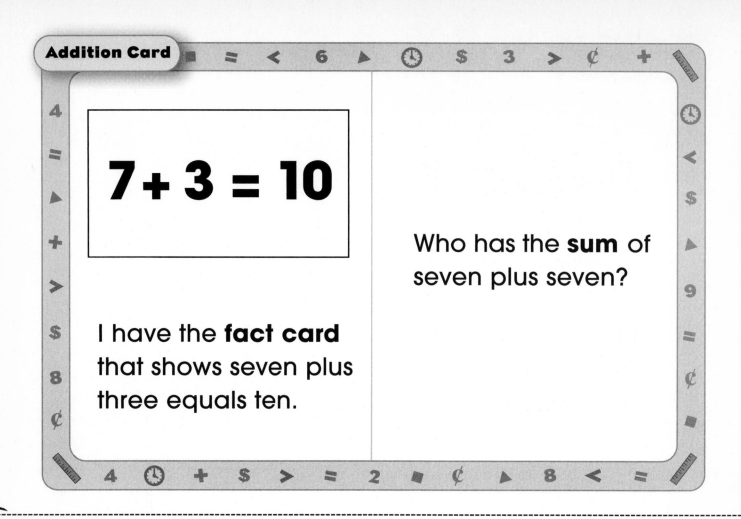

7 + 3 = 10

Who has the **sum** of seven plus seven?

I have the **fact card** that shows seven plus three equals ten.

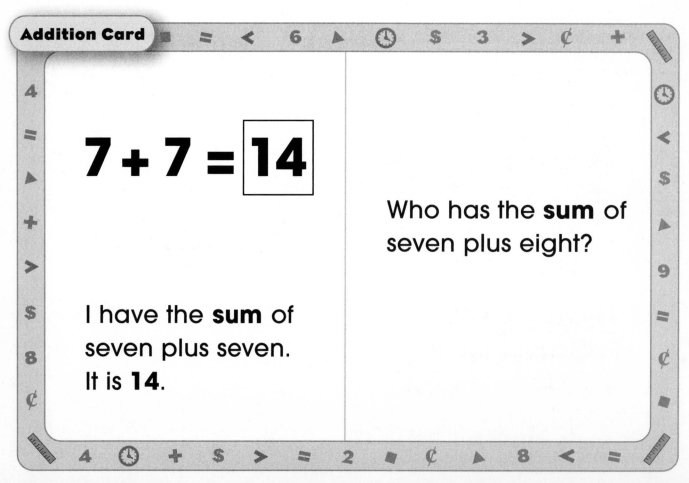

7 + 7 = 14

Who has the **sum** of seven plus eight?

I have the **sum** of seven plus seven. It is **14**.

Ask & Answer Interactive Math Practice: Grades 2–3 ©2007 by Joseph A. Porzio, Scholastic Teaching Resources

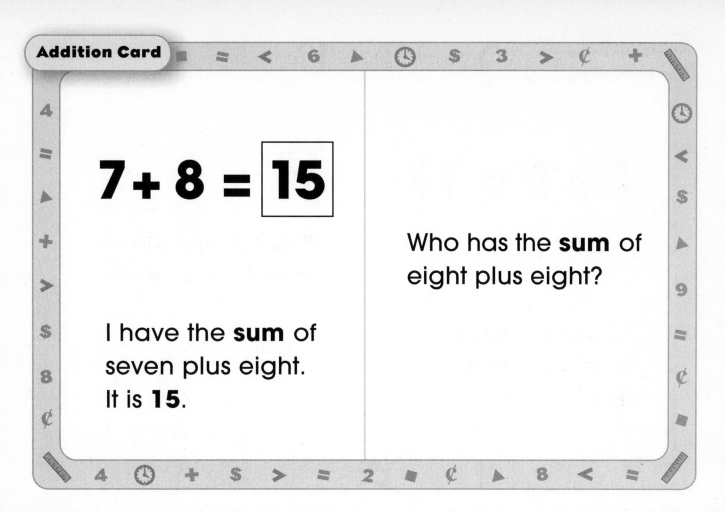

$$7 + 8 = \boxed{15}$$

Who has the **sum** of eight plus eight?

I have the **sum** of seven plus eight. It is **15**.

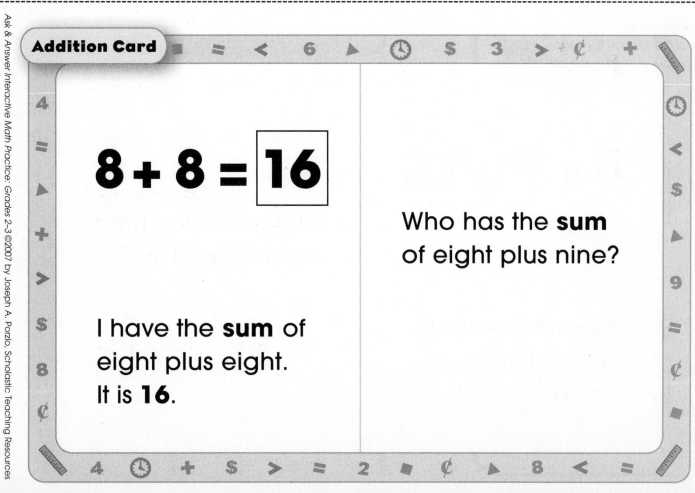

$$8 + 8 = \boxed{16}$$

Who has the **sum** of eight plus nine?

I have the **sum** of eight plus eight. It is **16**.

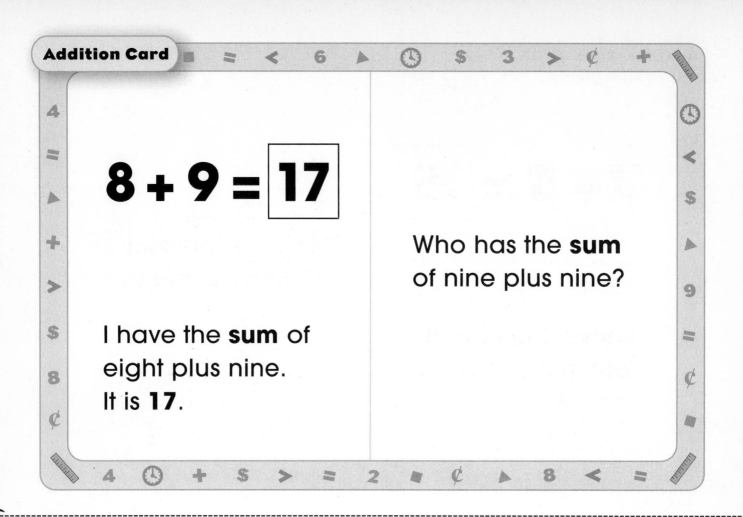

$$8 + 9 = \boxed{17}$$

I have the **sum** of
eight plus nine.
It is **17**.

Who has the **sum**
of nine plus nine?

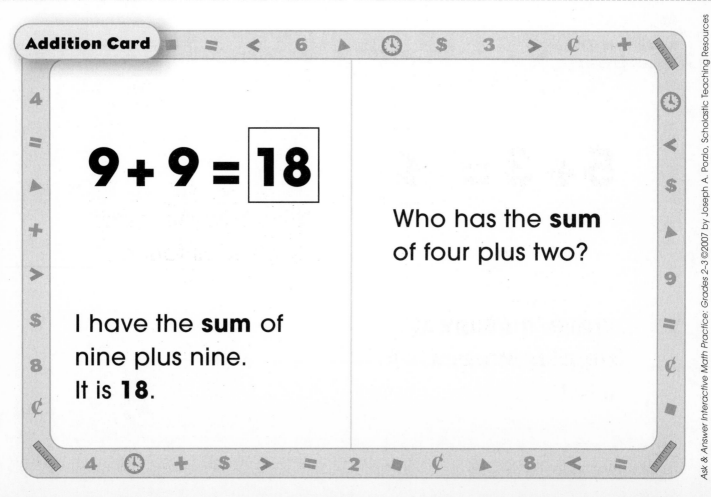

$$9 + 9 = \boxed{18}$$

I have the **sum** of
nine plus nine.
It is **18**.

Who has the **sum**
of four plus two?

Ask & Answer Interactive Math Practice: Grades 2–3 ©2007 by Joseph A. Porzio, Scholastic Teaching Resources

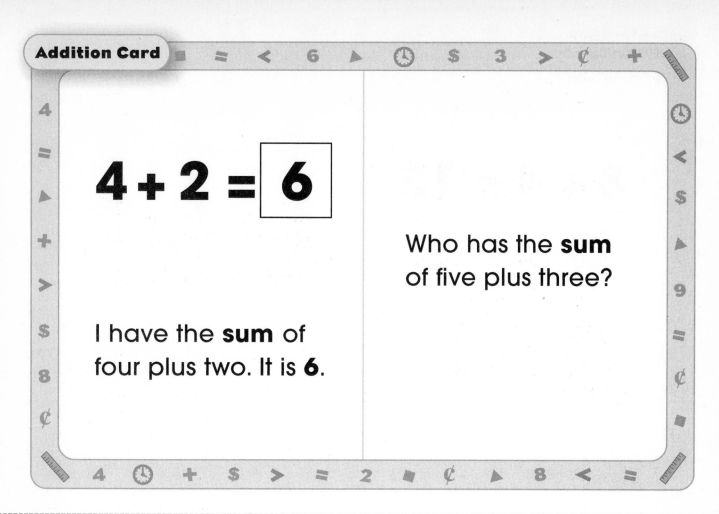

$$4 + 2 = \boxed{6}$$

Who has the **sum**
of five plus three?

I have the **sum** of
four plus two. It is **6**.

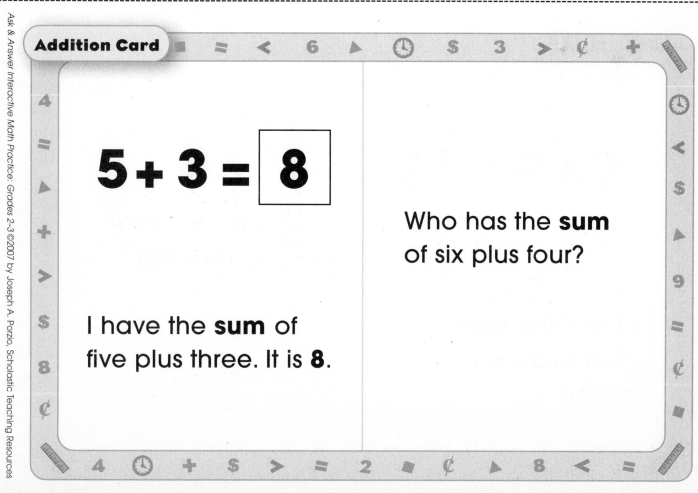

$$5 + 3 = \boxed{8}$$

Who has the **sum**
of six plus four?

I have the **sum** of
five plus three. It is **8**.

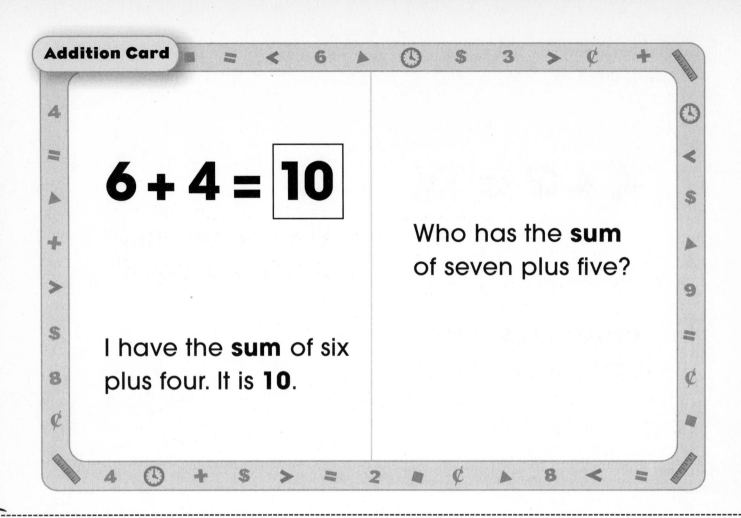

$$6 + 4 = \boxed{10}$$

Who has the **sum** of seven plus five?

I have the **sum** of six plus four. It is **10**.

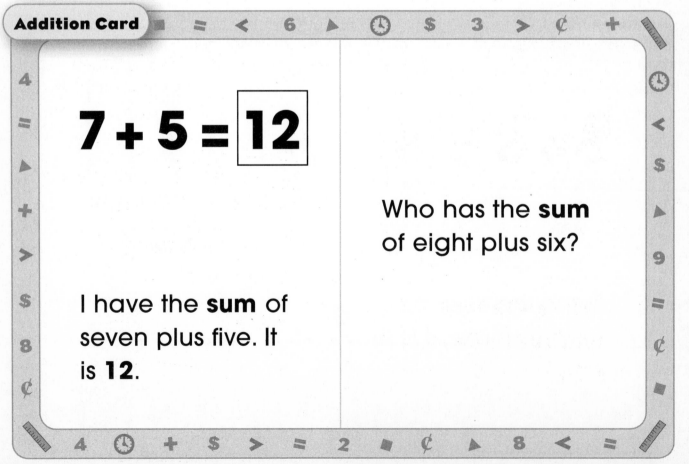

$$7 + 5 = \boxed{12}$$

Who has the **sum** of eight plus six?

I have the **sum** of seven plus five. It is **12**.

Ask & Answer Interactive Math Practice: Grades 2–3 ©2007 by Joseph A. Porzio, Scholastic Teaching Resources

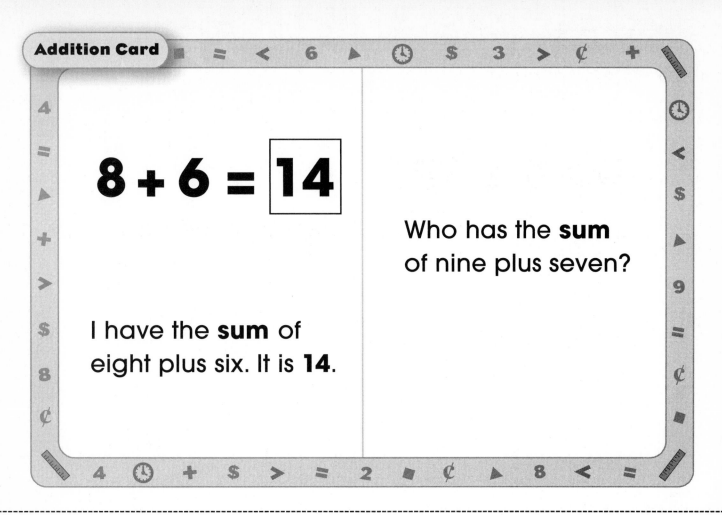

Addition Card

$$8 + 6 = \boxed{14}$$

Who has the **sum** of nine plus seven?

I have the **sum** of eight plus six. It is **14**.

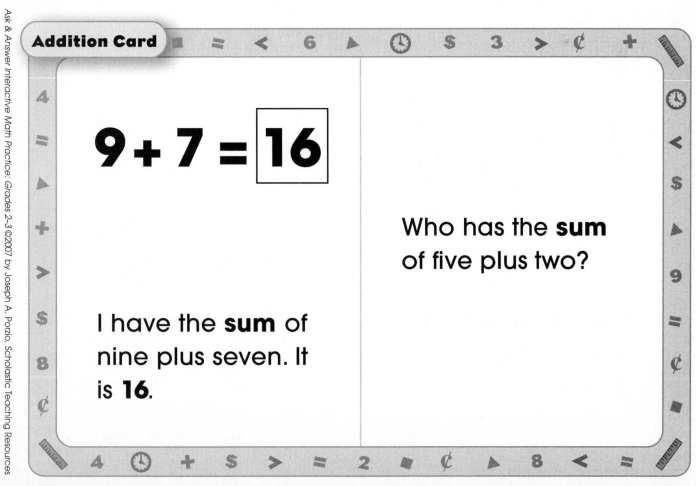

Addition Card

$$9 + 7 = \boxed{16}$$

Who has the **sum** of five plus two?

I have the **sum** of nine plus seven. It is **16**.

Ask & Answer Interactive Math Practice: Grades 2–3 ©2007 by Joseph A. Porzio, Scholastic Teaching Resources

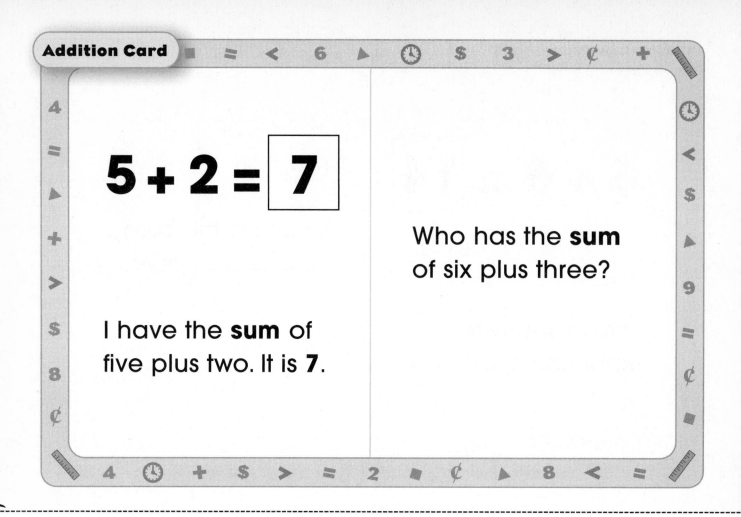

$$5 + 2 = \boxed{7}$$

Who has the **sum** of six plus three?

I have the **sum** of five plus two. It is **7**.

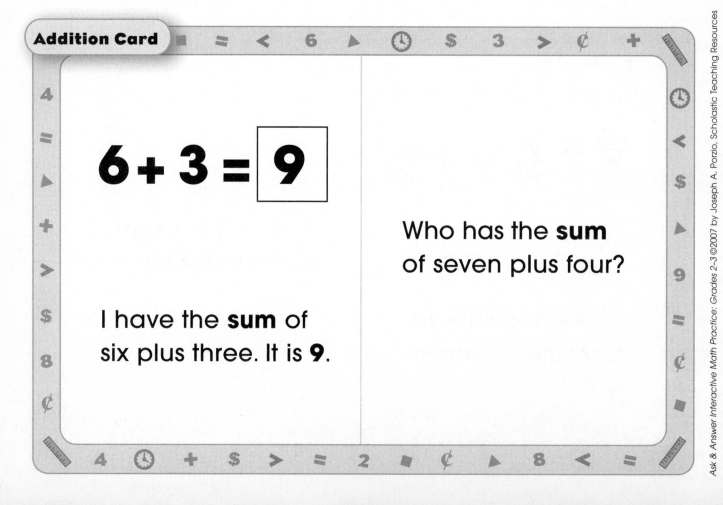

$$6 + 3 = \boxed{9}$$

Who has the **sum** of seven plus four?

I have the **sum** of six plus three. It is **9**.

20

Ask & Answer Interactive Math Practice: Grades 2–3 ©2007 by Joseph A. Porzio, Scholastic Teaching Resources

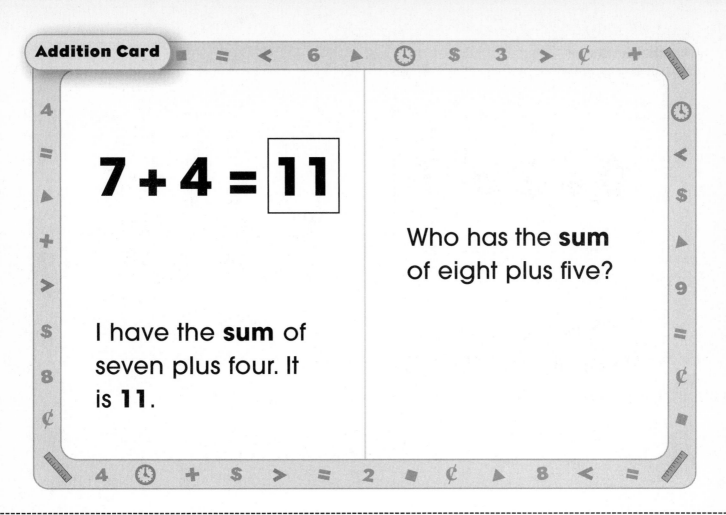

$7 + 4 = \boxed{11}$

Who has the **sum** of eight plus five?

I have the **sum** of seven plus four. It is **11**.

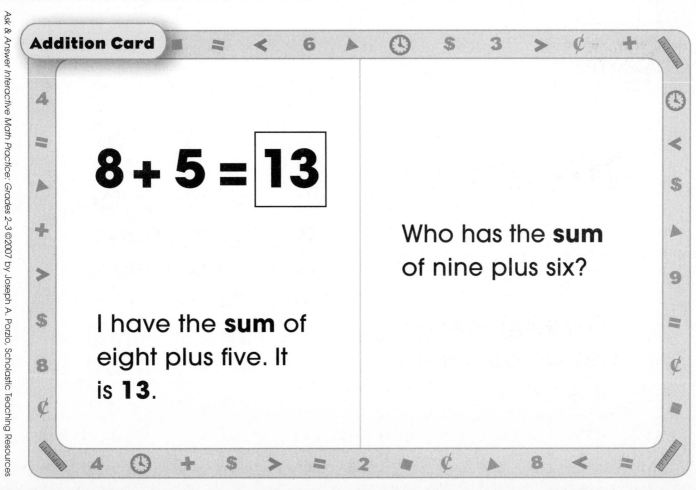

$8 + 5 = \boxed{13}$

Who has the **sum** of nine plus six?

I have the **sum** of eight plus five. It is **13**.

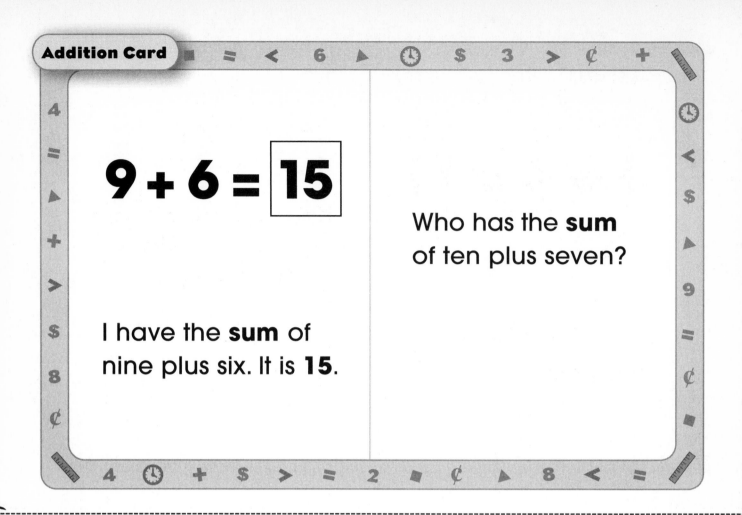

$$9 + 6 = \boxed{15}$$

Who has the **sum** of ten plus seven?

I have the **sum** of nine plus six. It is **15**.

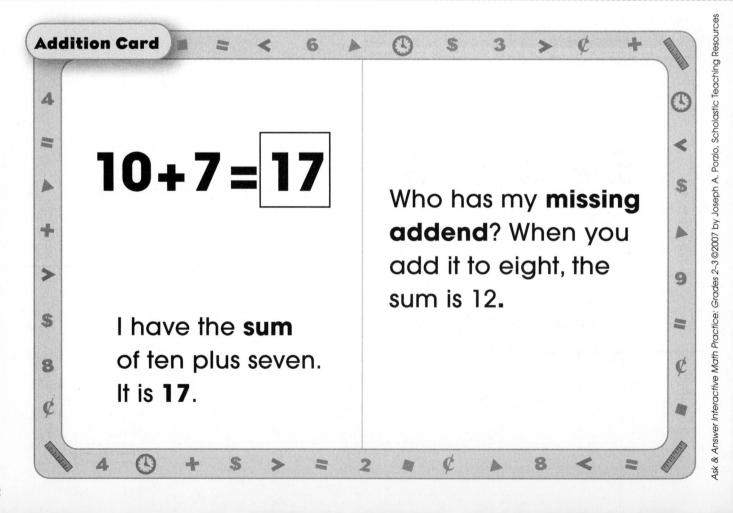

$$10 + 7 = \boxed{17}$$

Who has my **missing addend**? When you add it to eight, the sum is 12.

I have the **sum** of ten plus seven. It is **17**.

Ask & Answer Interactive Math Practice: Grades 2–3 ©2007 by Joseph A. Porzio, Scholastic Teaching Resources

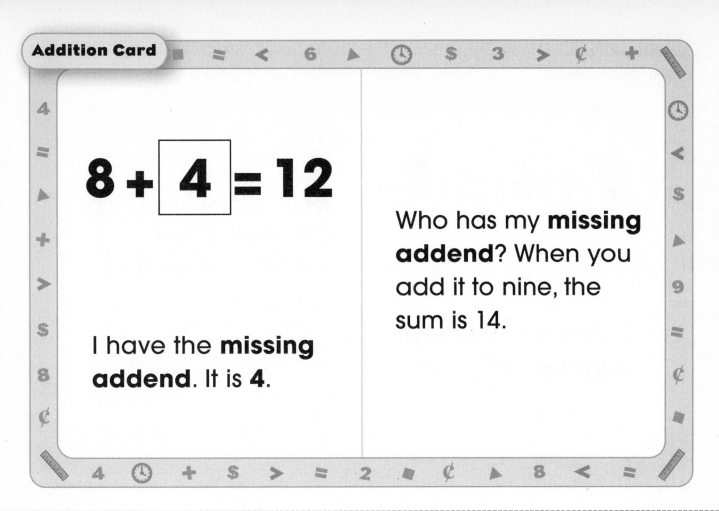

$$8 + \boxed{4} = 12$$

I have the **missing addend**. It is **4**.

Who has my **missing addend**? When you add it to nine, the sum is 14.

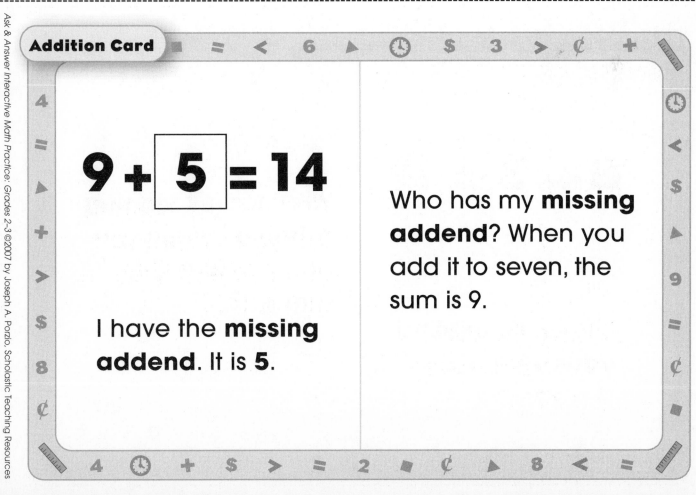

$$9 + \boxed{5} = 14$$

I have the **missing addend**. It is **5**.

Who has my **missing addend**? When you add it to seven, the sum is 9.

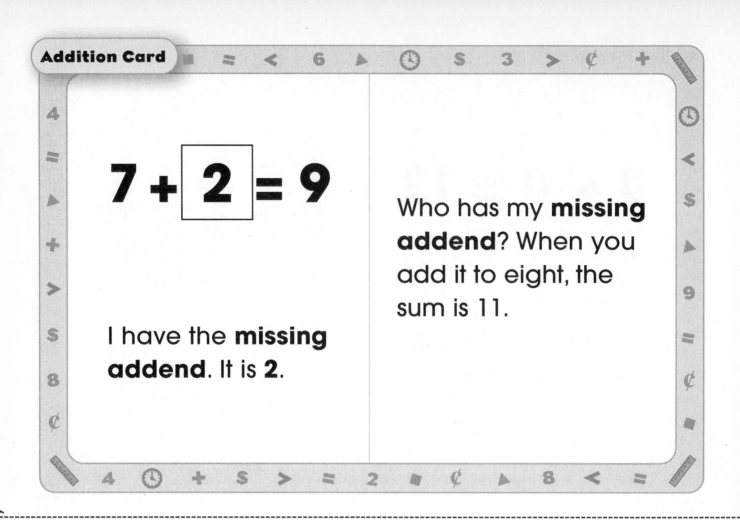

$$7 + \boxed{2} = 9$$

Who has my **missing addend**? When you add it to eight, the sum is 11.

I have the **missing addend**. It is **2**.

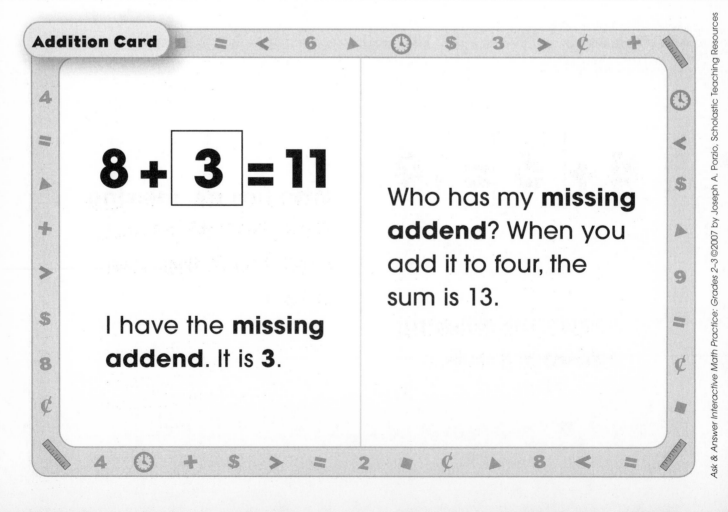

$$8 + \boxed{3} = 11$$

Who has my **missing addend**? When you add it to four, the sum is 13.

I have the **missing addend**. It is **3**.

Ask & Answer Interactive Math Practice: Grades 2–3 ©2007 by Joseph A. Porzio, Scholastic Teaching Resources

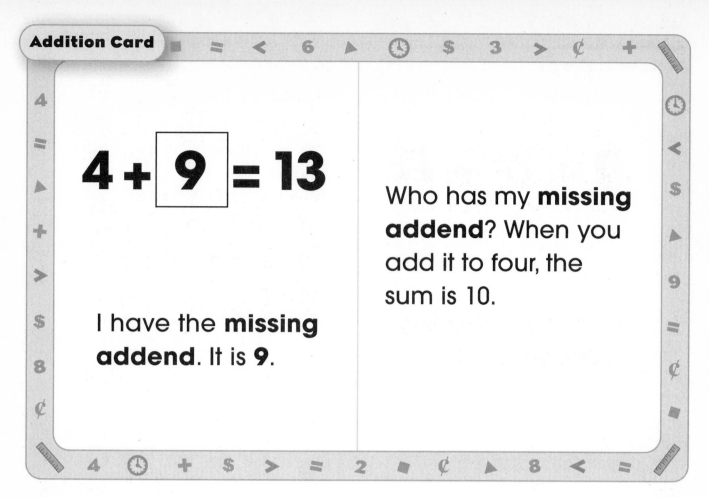

Addition Card

$$4 + \boxed{9} = 13$$

I have the **missing addend**. It is **9**.

Who has my **missing addend**? When you add it to four, the sum is 10.

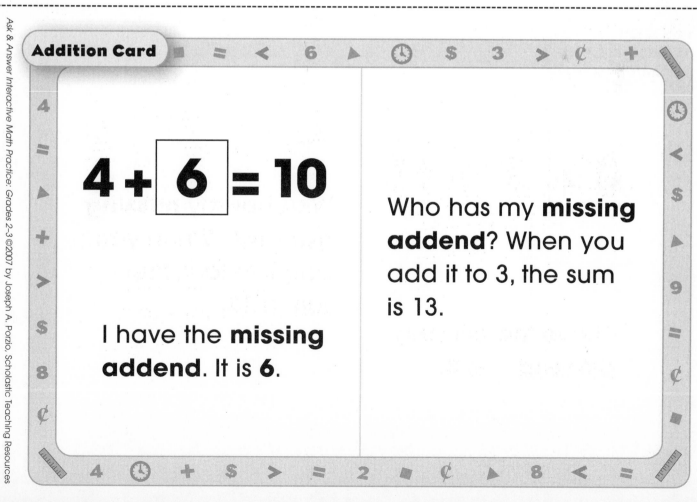

Addition Card

$$4 + \boxed{6} = 10$$

I have the **missing addend**. It is **6**.

Who has my **missing addend**? When you add it to 3, the sum is 13.

Ask & Answer Interactive Math Practice: Grades 2–3 ©2007 by Joseph A. Porzio, Scholastic Teaching Resources

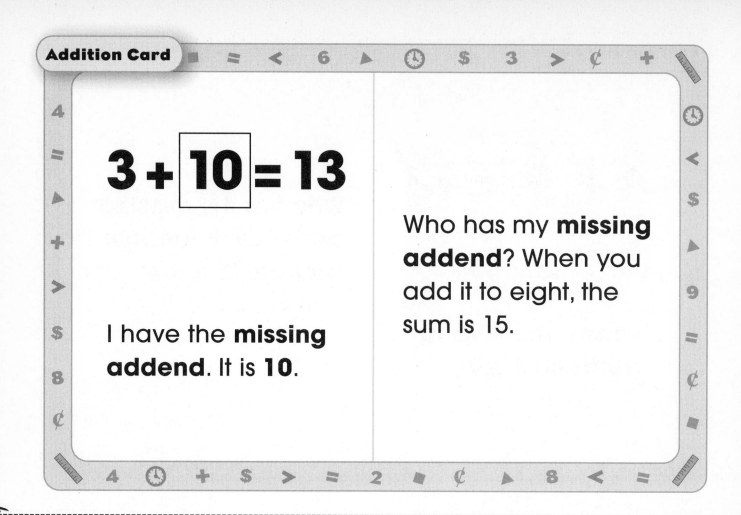

$$3 + \boxed{10} = 13$$

I have the **missing addend**. It is **10**.

Who has my **missing addend**? When you add it to eight, the sum is 15.

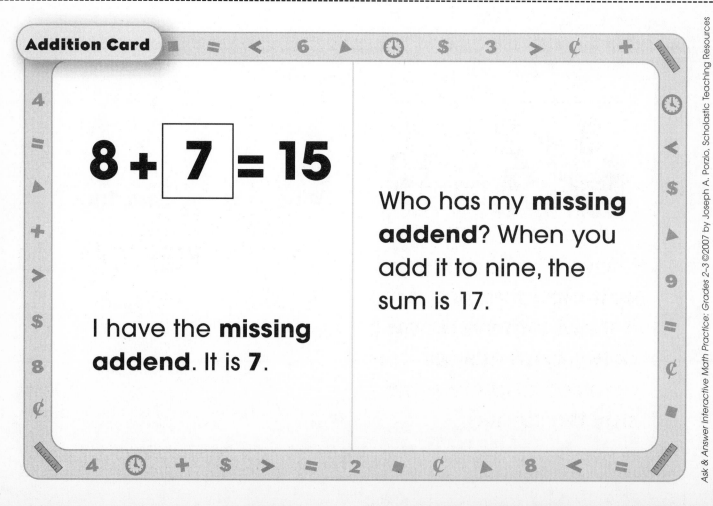

$$8 + \boxed{7} = 15$$

I have the **missing addend**. It is **7**.

Who has my **missing addend**? When you add it to nine, the sum is 17.

Ask & Answer Interactive Math Practice: Grades 2–3 ©2007 by Joseph A. Porzio, Scholastic Teaching Resources

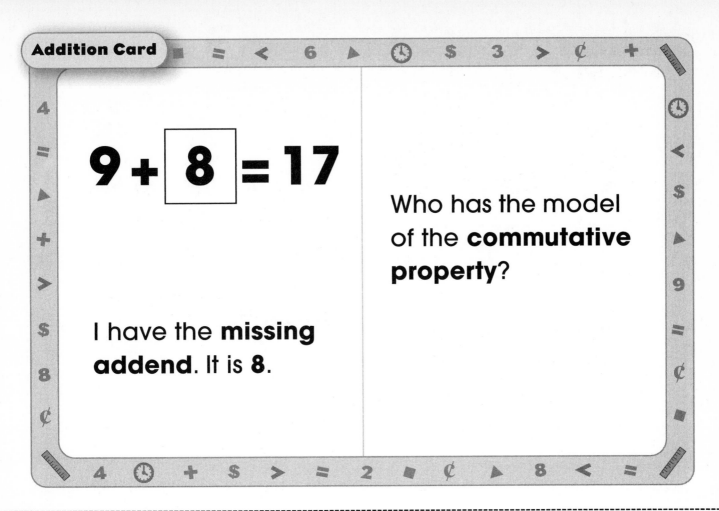

$$9 + \boxed{8} = 17$$

Who has the model of the **commutative property**?

I have the **missing addend**. It is **8**.

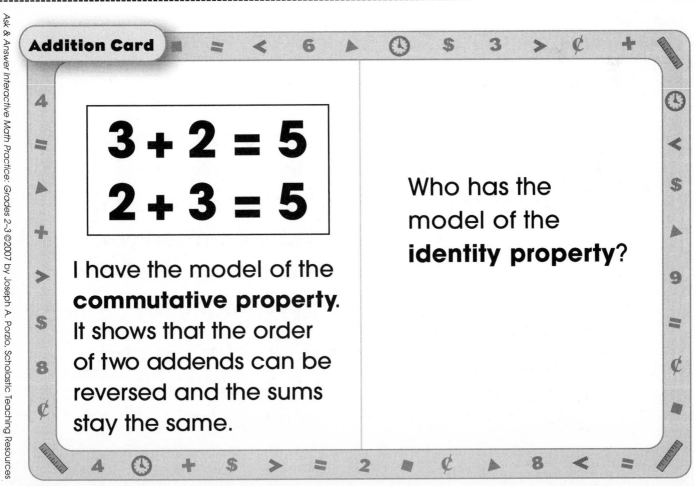

$$3 + 2 = 5$$
$$2 + 3 = 5$$

Who has the model of the **identity property**?

I have the model of the **commutative property**. It shows that the order of two addends can be reversed and the sums stay the same.

$$8 + 0 = 8$$
$$0 + 6 = 6$$

I have the model of the **identity property**. It shows that when zero (0) is added to any number (addend), the number stays the same.

Who has the model that shows **how addition and subtraction are related**?

$$3 + 2 = 5$$
$$5 - 2 = 3$$

I have the model that shows **how addition and subtraction are related**.

Who can go to the board to model and explain one of the following?

- **The Commutative Property of Addition**
- **The Identity Property**
- **How addition and subtraction are related**

Ask & Answer Interactive Math Practice: Grades 2–3 ©2007 by Joseph A. Porzio, Scholastic Teaching Resources

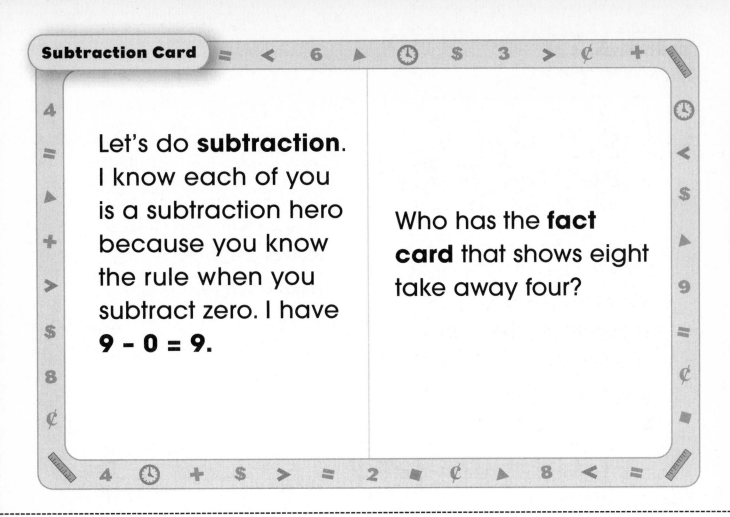

Let's do **subtraction**. I know each of you is a subtraction hero because you know the rule when you subtract zero. I have **9 – 0 = 9.**

Who has the **fact card** that shows eight take away four?

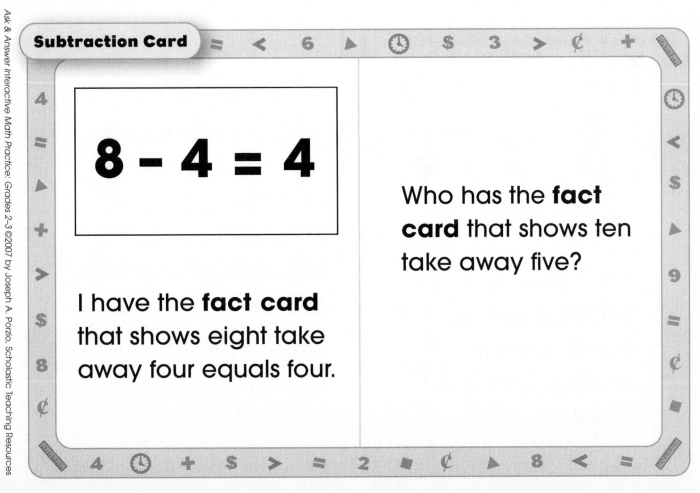

$$8 - 4 = 4$$

I have the **fact card** that shows eight take away four equals four.

Who has the **fact card** that shows ten take away five?

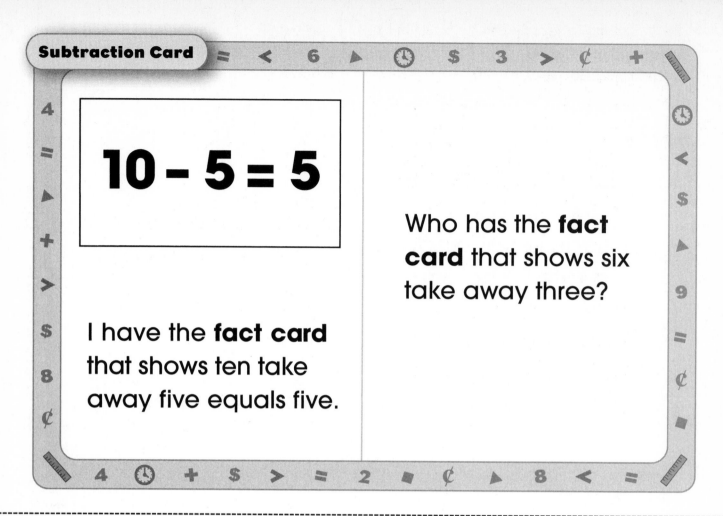

10 – 5 = 5

Who has the **fact card** that shows six take away three?

I have the **fact card** that shows ten take away five equals five.

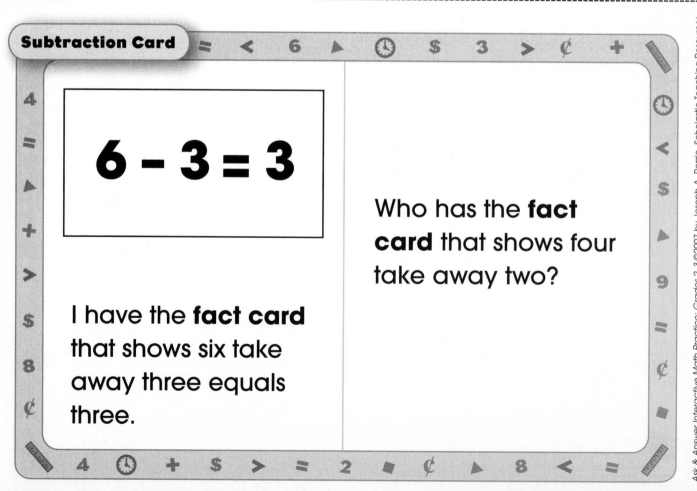

6 – 3 = 3

Who has the **fact card** that shows four take away two?

I have the **fact card** that shows six take away three equals three.

Ask & Answer Interactive Math Practice: Grades 2–3 ©2007 by Joseph A. Porzio. Scholastic Teaching Resources

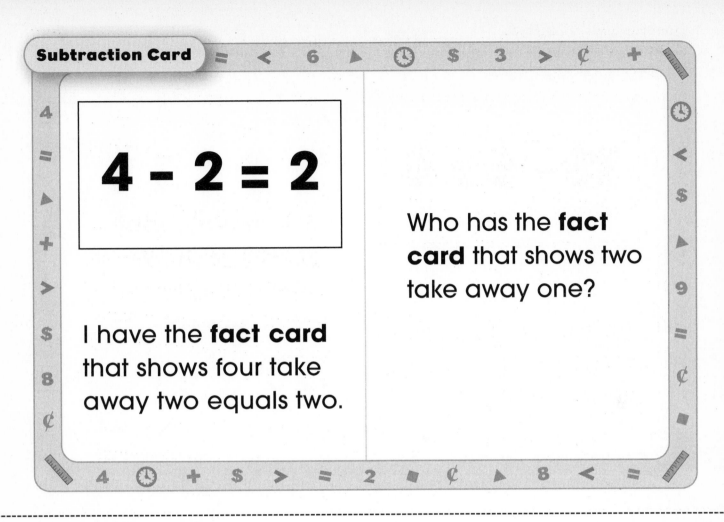

Subtraction Card

$$4 - 2 = 2$$

Who has the **fact card** that shows two take away one?

I have the **fact card** that shows four take away two equals two.

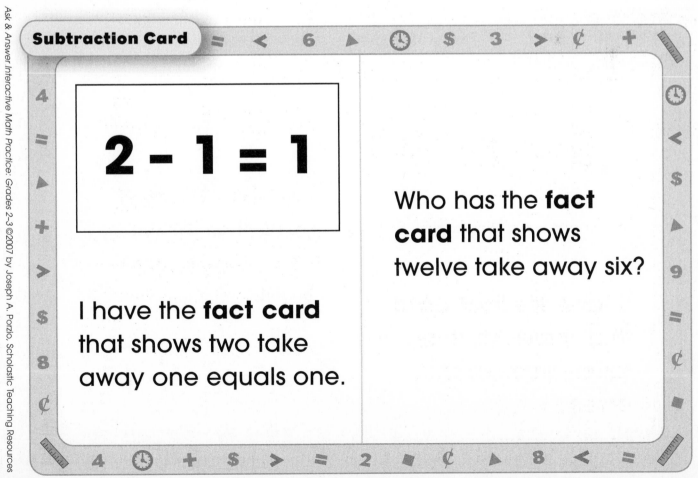

Subtraction Card

$$2 - 1 = 1$$

Who has the **fact card** that shows twelve take away six?

I have the **fact card** that shows two take away one equals one.

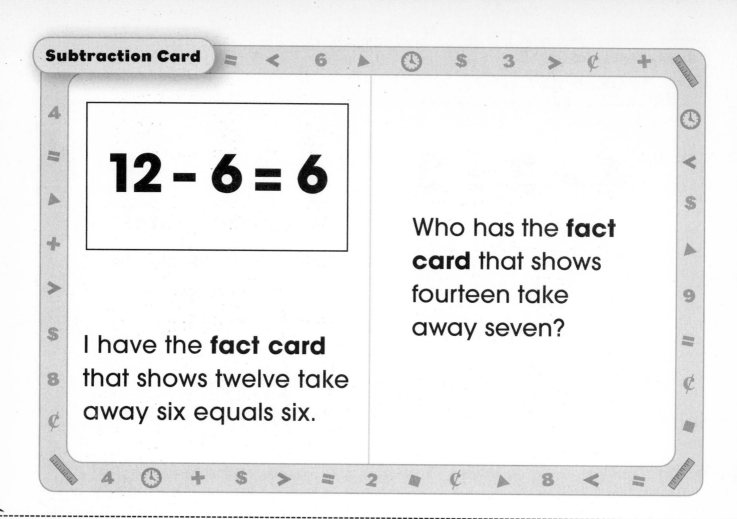

12 − 6 = 6

I have the **fact card** that shows twelve take away six equals six.

Who has the **fact card** that shows fourteen take away seven?

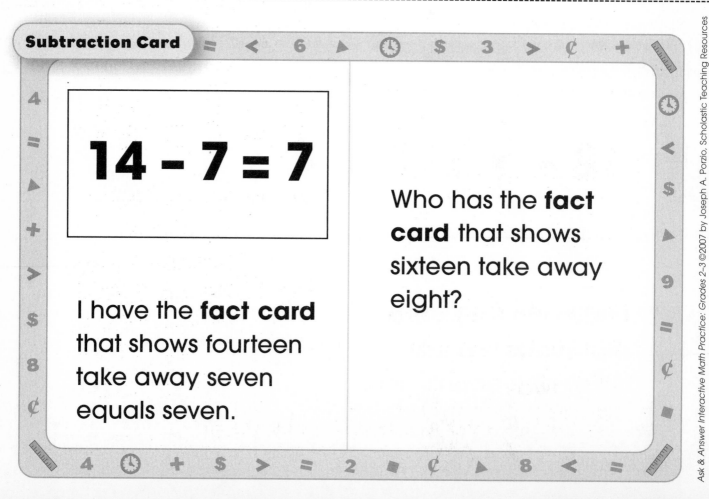

14 − 7 = 7

I have the **fact card** that shows fourteen take away seven equals seven.

Who has the **fact card** that shows sixteen take away eight?

Ask & Answer Interactive Math Practice: Grades 2–3 ©2007 by Joseph A. Porzio, Scholastic Teaching Resources

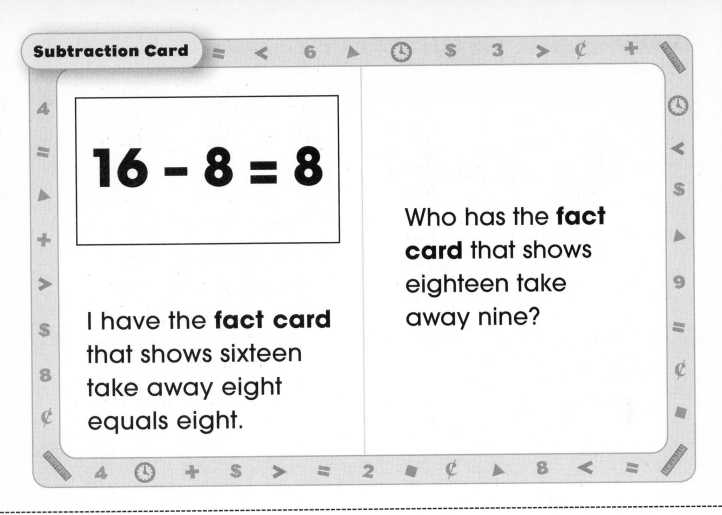

16 – 8 = 8

I have the **fact card** that shows sixteen take away eight equals eight.

Who has the **fact card** that shows eighteen take away nine?

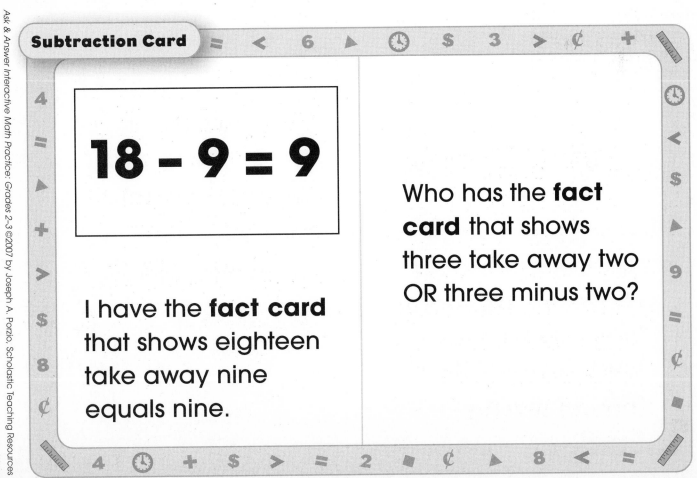

18 – 9 = 9

I have the **fact card** that shows eighteen take away nine equals nine.

Who has the **fact card** that shows three take away two OR three minus two?

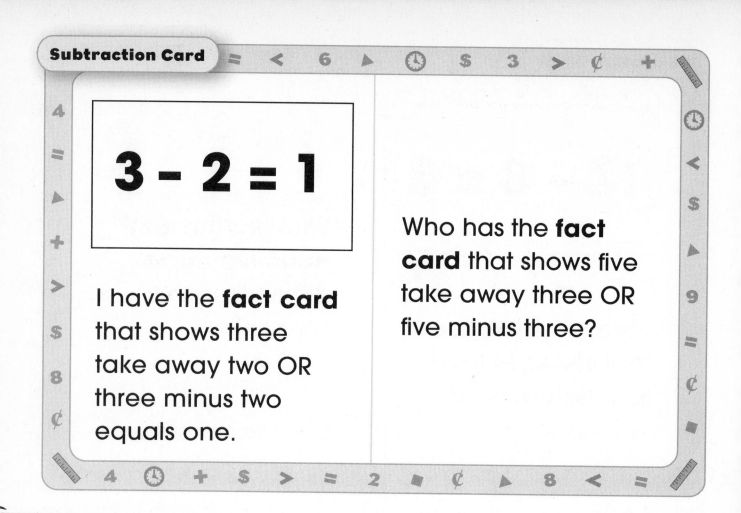

$$3 - 2 = 1$$

I have the **fact card** that shows three take away two OR three minus two equals one.

Who has the **fact card** that shows five take away three OR five minus three?

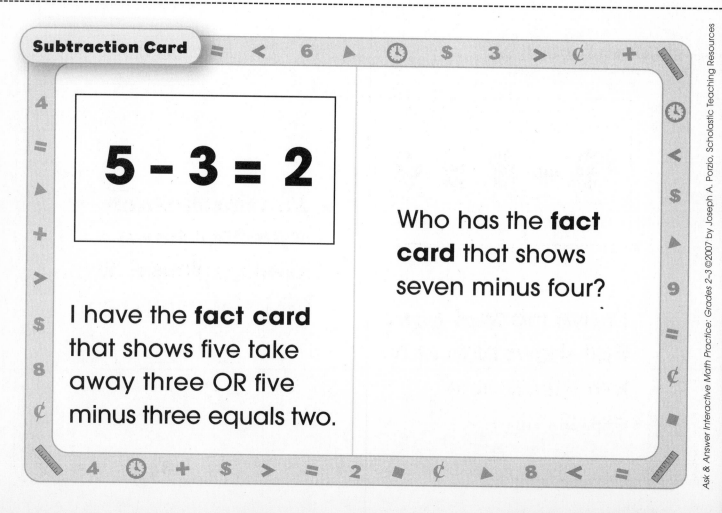

$$5 - 3 = 2$$

I have the **fact card** that shows five take away three OR five minus three equals two.

Who has the **fact card** that shows seven minus four?

Ask & Answer Interactive Math Practice: Grades 2–3 ©2007 by Joseph A. Porzio, Scholastic Teaching Resources

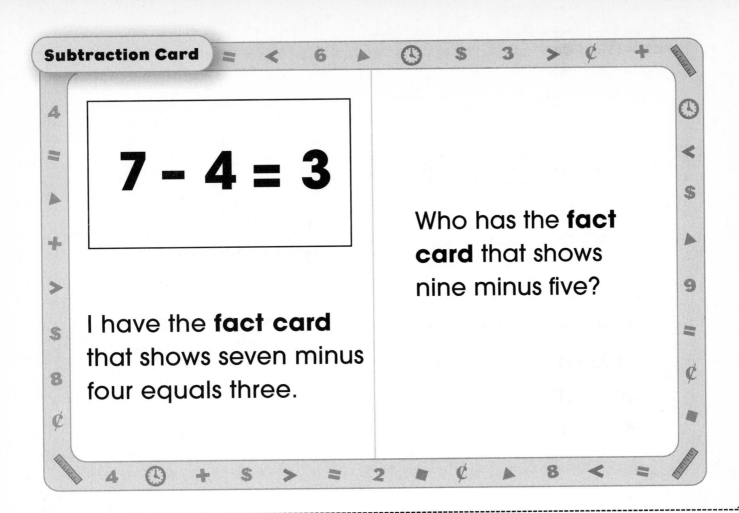

7 - 4 = 3

I have the **fact card** that shows seven minus four equals three.

Who has the **fact card** that shows nine minus five?

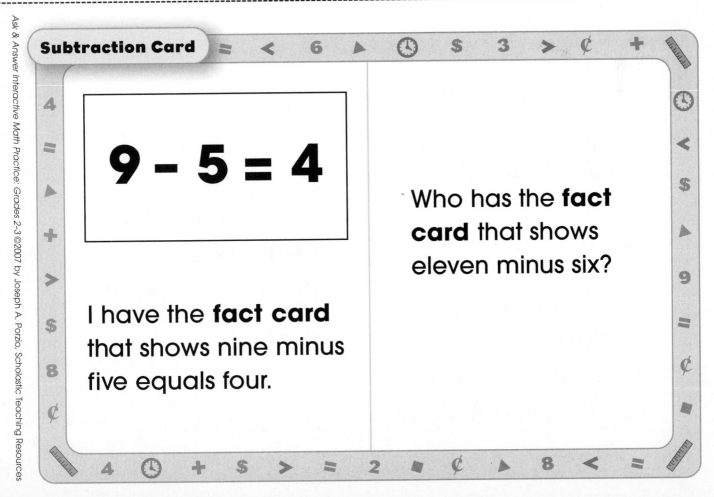

9 - 5 = 4

I have the **fact card** that shows nine minus five equals four.

Who has the **fact card** that shows eleven minus six?

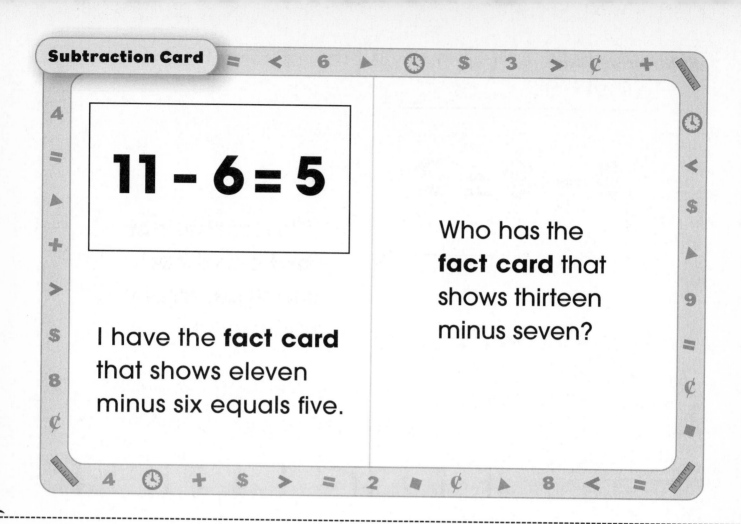

= < 6 ▶ 🕐 $ 3 > ¢ +

11 − 6 = 5

I have the **fact card** that shows eleven minus six equals five.

Who has the **fact card** that shows thirteen minus seven?

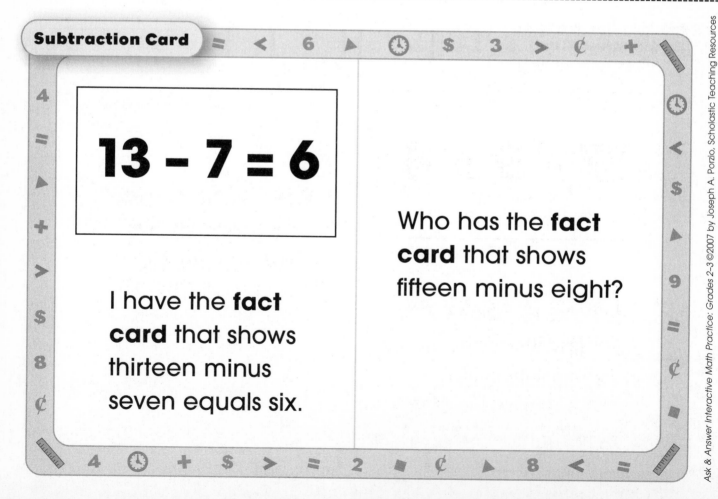

= < 6 ▶ 🕐 $ 3 > ¢ +

13 − 7 = 6

I have the **fact card** that shows thirteen minus seven equals six.

Who has the **fact card** that shows fifteen minus eight?

Ask & Answer Interactive Math Practice: Grades 2–3 ©2007 by Joseph A. Porzio, Scholastic Teaching Resources

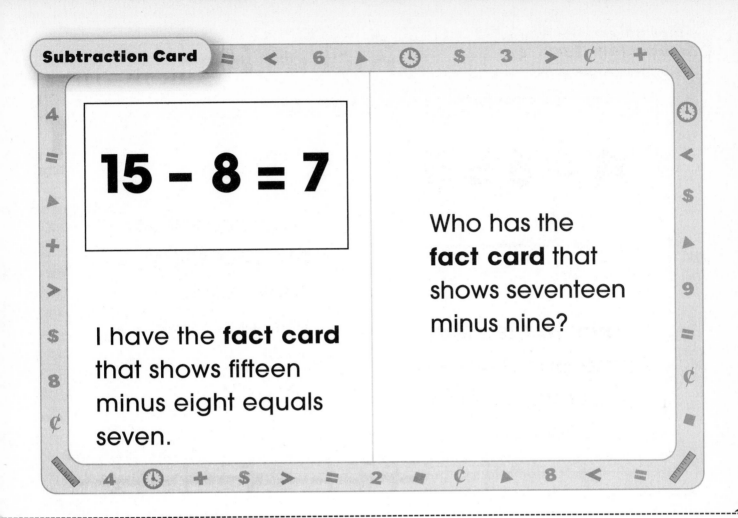

Subtraction Card

15 – 8 = 7

I have the **fact card** that shows fifteen minus eight equals seven.

Who has the **fact card** that shows seventeen minus nine?

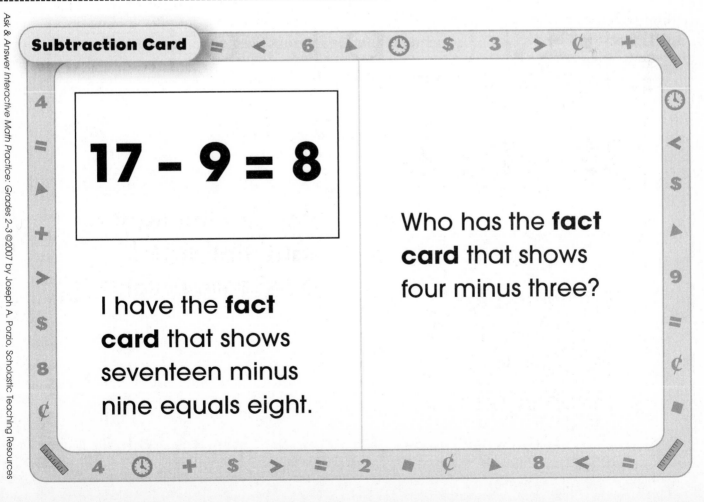

Subtraction Card

17 – 9 = 8

I have the **fact card** that shows seventeen minus nine equals eight.

Who has the **fact card** that shows four minus three?

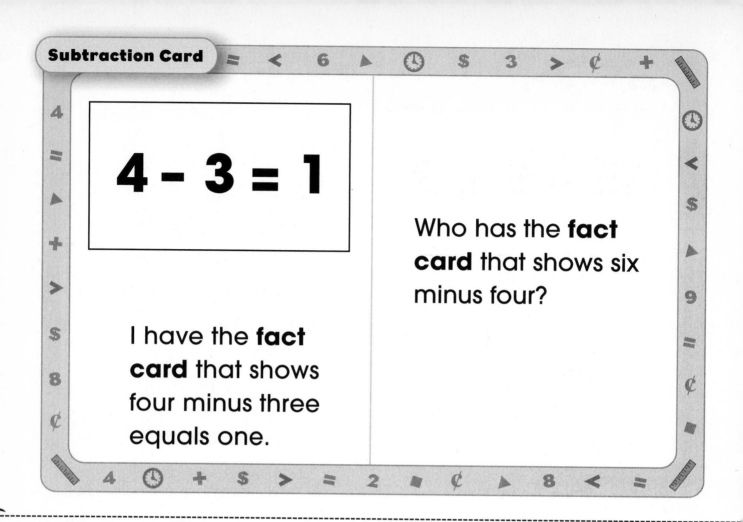

4 − 3 = 1

I have the **fact card** that shows four minus three equals one.

Who has the **fact card** that shows six minus four?

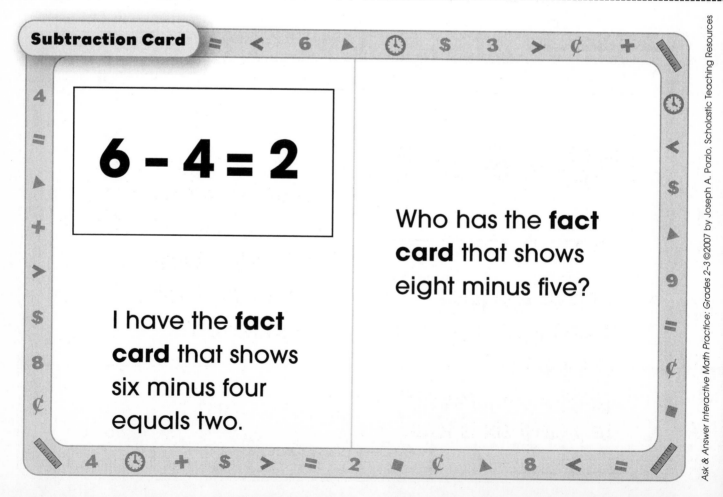

6 − 4 = 2

I have the **fact card** that shows six minus four equals two.

Who has the **fact card** that shows eight minus five?

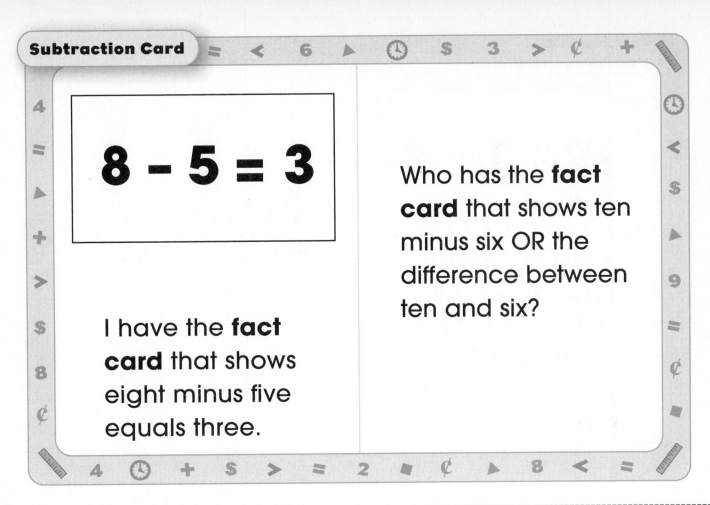

8 − 5 = 3

I have the **fact card** that shows eight minus five equals three.

Who has the **fact card** that shows ten minus six OR the difference between ten and six?

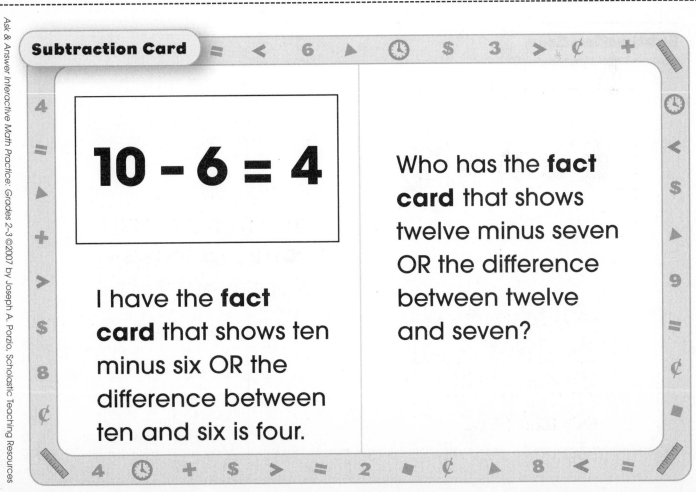

10 − 6 = 4

I have the **fact card** that shows ten minus six OR the difference between ten and six is four.

Who has the **fact card** that shows twelve minus seven OR the difference between twelve and seven?

$$12 - 7 = 5$$

I have the **fact card** that shows twelve minus seven OR the difference between twelve and seven is five.

Who has the **difference** between fourteen and eight?

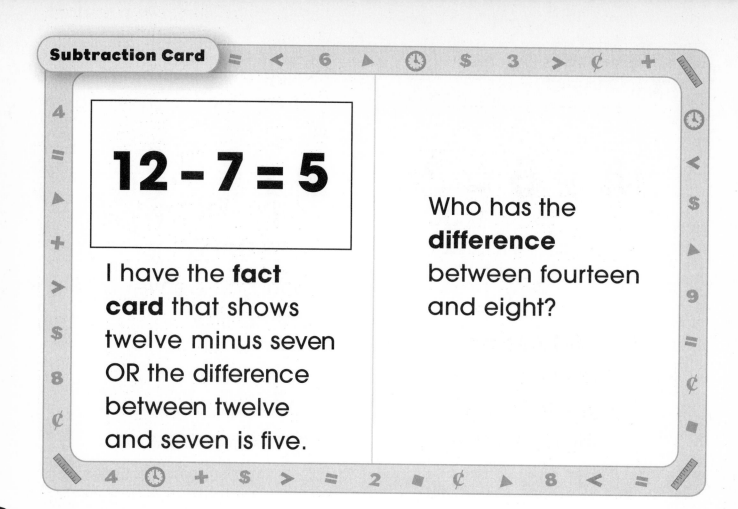

$$14 - 8 = \boxed{6}$$

I have the **difference** between fourteen and eight. It is **6**.

Who has the **difference** between sixteen and nine?

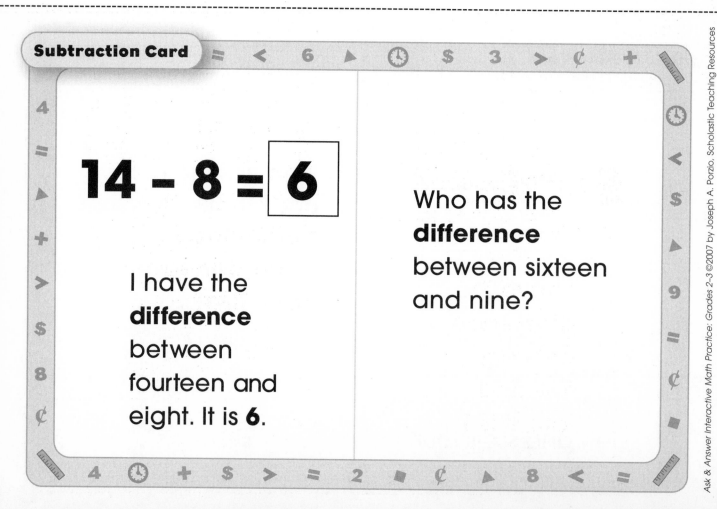

Ask & Answer Interactive Math Practice: Grades 2–3 ©2007 by Joseph A. Porzio, Scholastic Teaching Resources

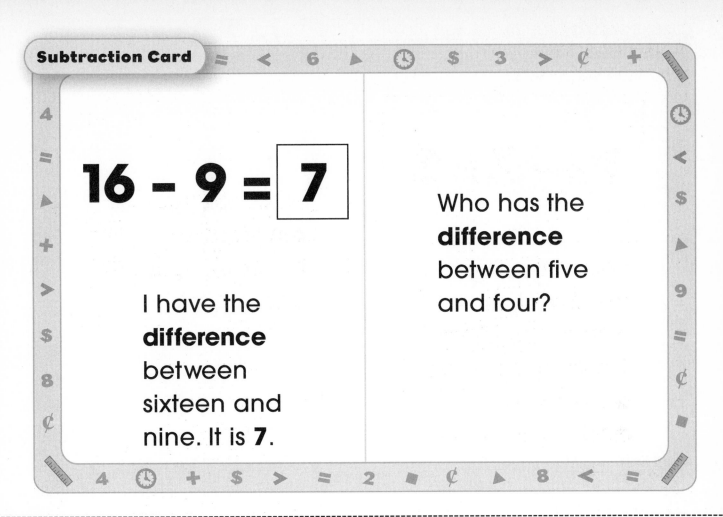

$16 - 9 = \boxed{7}$

I have the **difference** between sixteen and nine. It is **7**.

Who has the **difference** between five and four?

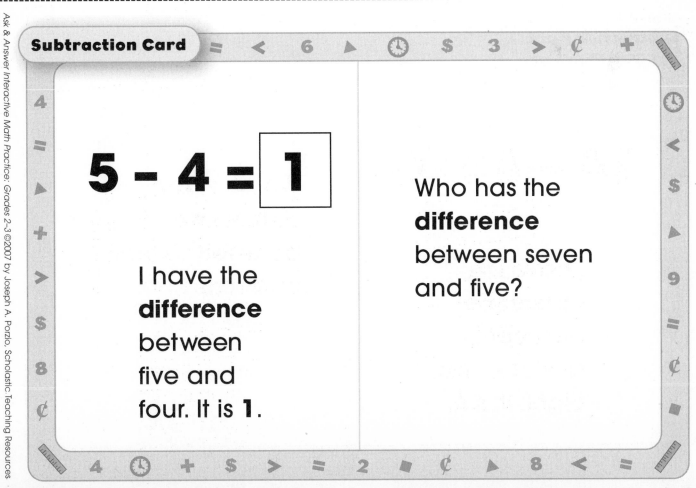

$5 - 4 = \boxed{1}$

I have the **difference** between five and four. It is **1**.

Who has the **difference** between seven and five?

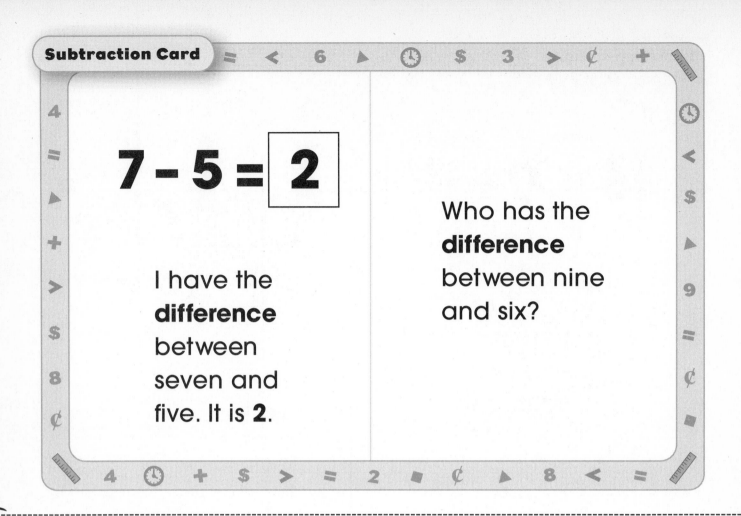

$$7 - 5 = \boxed{2}$$

I have the **difference** between seven and five. It is **2**.

Who has the **difference** between nine and six?

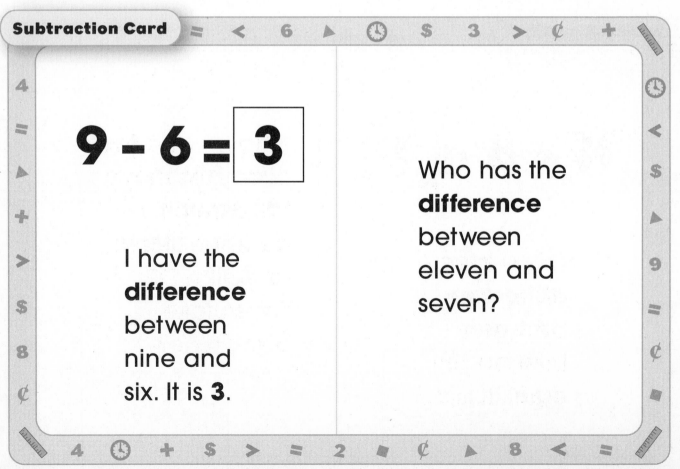

$$9 - 6 = \boxed{3}$$

I have the **difference** between nine and six. It is **3**.

Who has the **difference** between eleven and seven?

Ask & Answer Interactive Math Practice: Grades 2–3 ©2007 by Joseph A. Porzio, Scholastic Teaching Resources

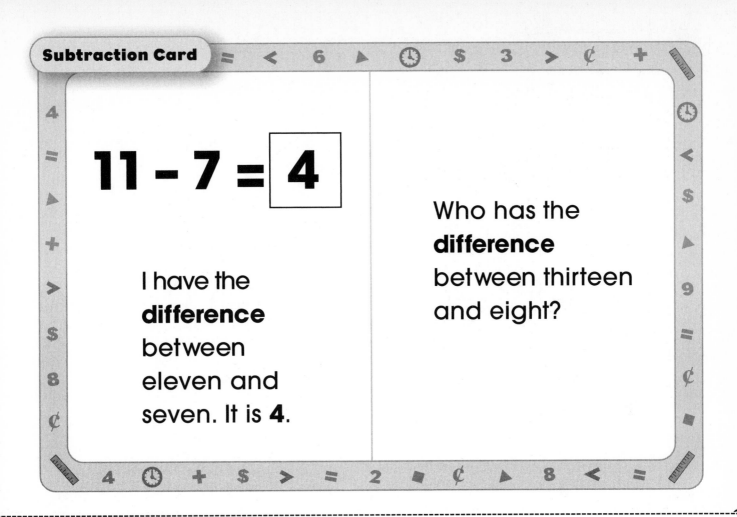

11 - 7 = 4

I have the **difference** between eleven and seven. It is **4**.

Who has the **difference** between thirteen and eight?

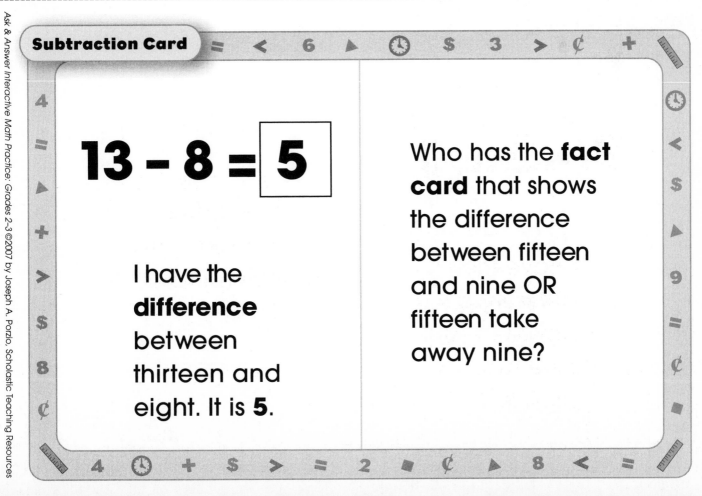

13 - 8 = 5

I have the **difference** between thirteen and eight. It is **5**.

Who has the **fact card** that shows the difference between fifteen and nine OR fifteen take away nine?

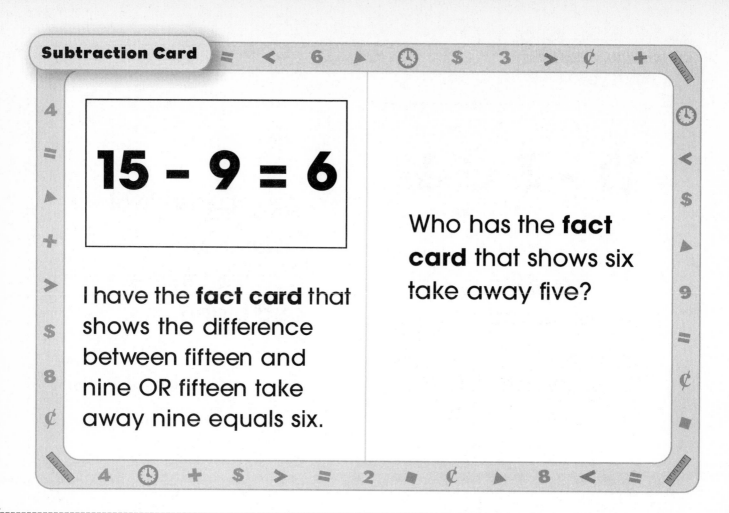

15 − 9 = 6

I have the **fact card** that shows the difference between fifteen and nine OR fifteen take away nine equals six.

Who has the **fact card** that shows six take away five?

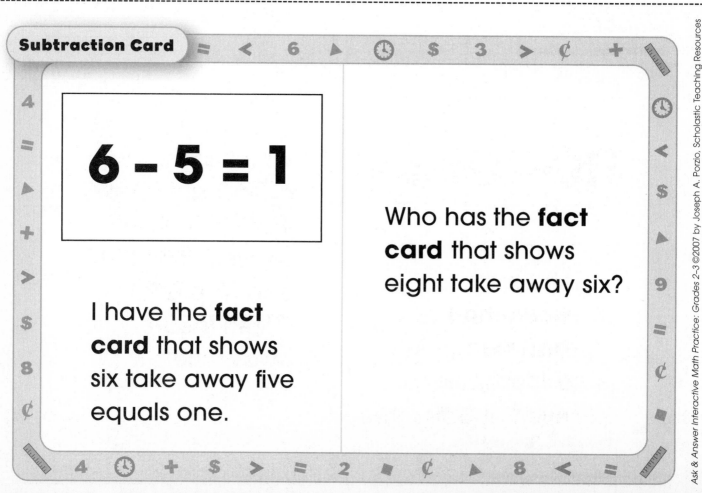

6 − 5 = 1

I have the **fact card** that shows six take away five equals one.

Who has the **fact card** that shows eight take away six?

Ask & Answer Interactive Math Practice: Grades 2–3 ©2007 by Joseph A. Porzio, Scholastic Teaching Resources

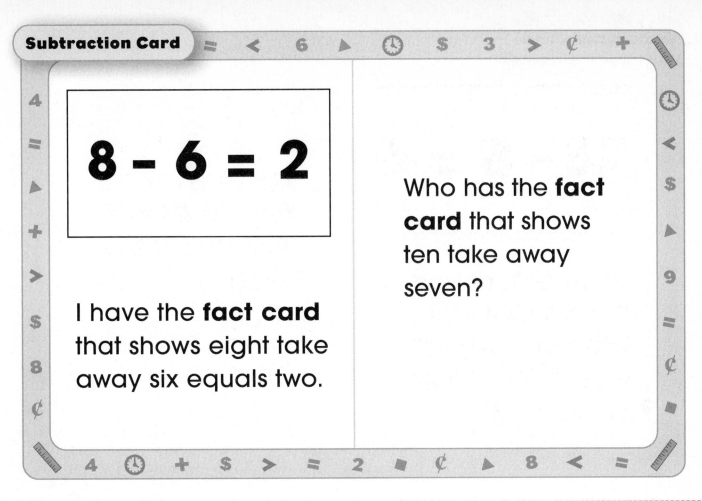

8 – 6 = 2

I have the **fact card** that shows eight take away six equals two.

Who has the **fact card** that shows ten take away seven?

Ask & Answer Interactive Math Practice: Grades 2–3 ©2007 by Joseph A. Porzio, Scholastic Teaching Resources

Subtraction Card

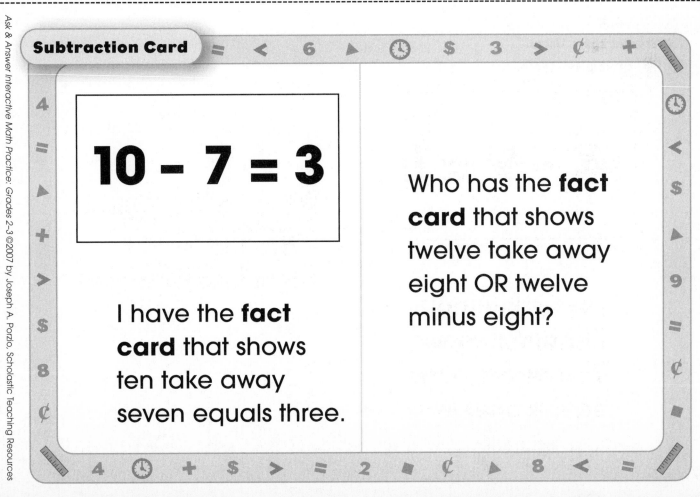

10 – 7 = 3

I have the **fact card** that shows ten take away seven equals three.

Who has the **fact card** that shows twelve take away eight OR twelve minus eight?

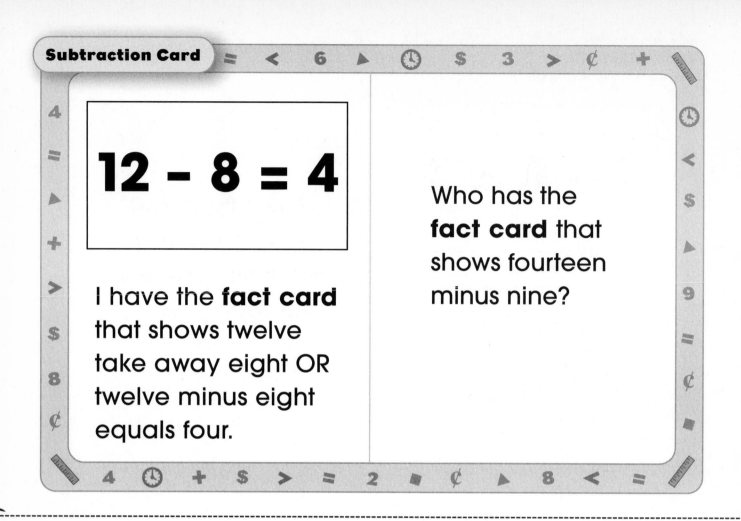

12 − 8 = 4

I have the **fact card** that shows twelve take away eight OR twelve minus eight equals four.

Who has the **fact card** that shows fourteen minus nine?

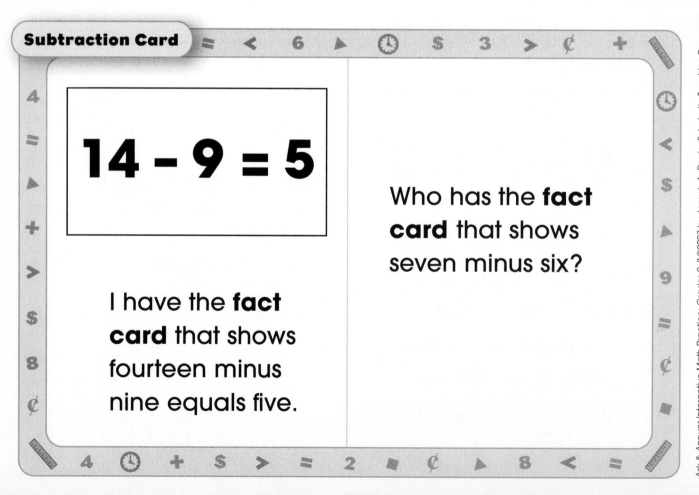

14 − 9 = 5

I have the **fact card** that shows fourteen minus nine equals five.

Who has the **fact card** that shows seven minus six?

Ask & Answer Interactive Math Practice: Grades 2–3 ©2007 by Joseph A. Porzio, Scholastic Teaching Resources

Ask & Answer Interactive Math Practice: Grades 2–3 ©2007 by Joseph A. Porzio. Scholastic Teaching Resources

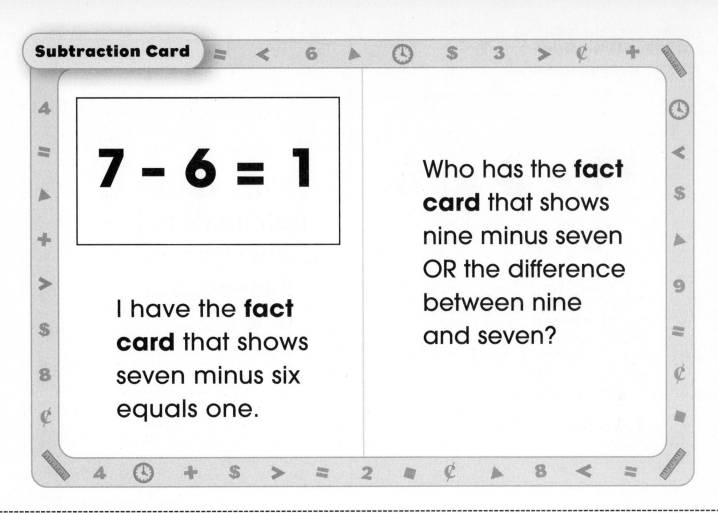

Subtraction Card

$$7 - 6 = 1$$

I have the **fact card** that shows seven minus six equals one.

Who has the **fact card** that shows nine minus seven OR the difference between nine and seven?

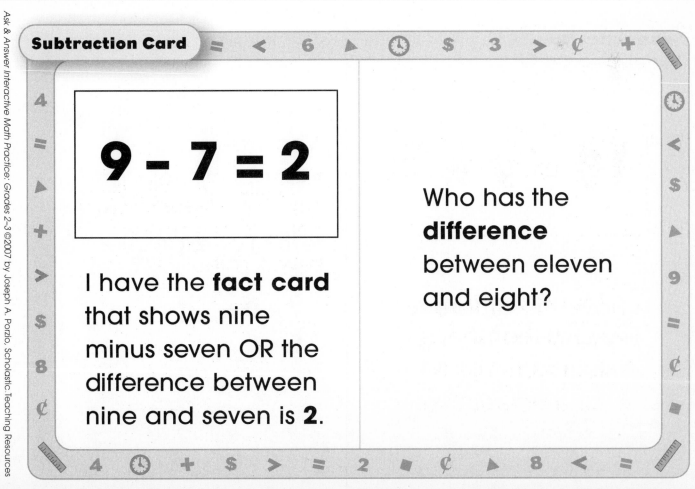

Subtraction Card

$$9 - 7 = 2$$

I have the **fact card** that shows nine minus seven OR the difference between nine and seven is **2**.

Who has the **difference** between eleven and eight?

11 - 8 = 3

I have the **difference** between eleven and eight. It is **3**.

Who has the **difference** between thirteen and nine?

13 - 9 = 4

I have the **difference** between thirteen and nine. It is **4**.

Who wants to be a subtraction hero and tell us the **rule about zero**? For example:

5 - 0 = ____
7 - 0 = ____
8 - 0 = ____

Ask & Answer Interactive Math Practice: Grades 2–3 ©2007 by Joseph A. Porzio. Scholastic Teaching Resources

Let's begin our **money** review about coins and bills and more. I have a coin that is worth one cent. On it you'll find a president.

Who has the **coin** that is worth one cent? It has a picture of a president.

Money Card

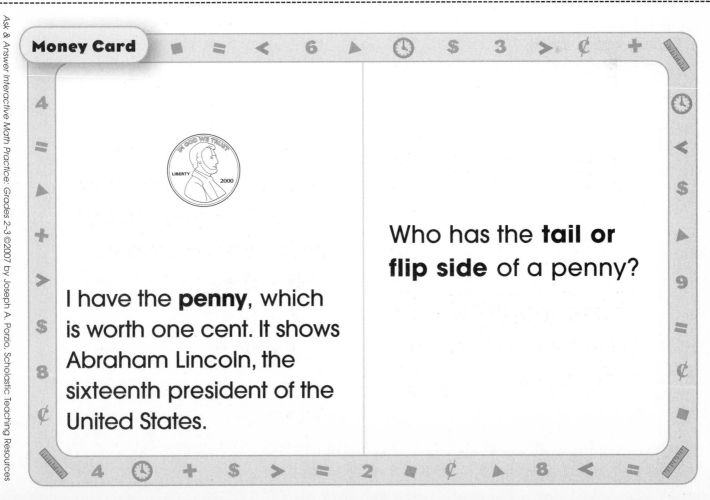

I have the **penny**, which is worth one cent. It shows Abraham Lincoln, the sixteenth president of the United States.

Who has the **tail or flip side** of a penny?

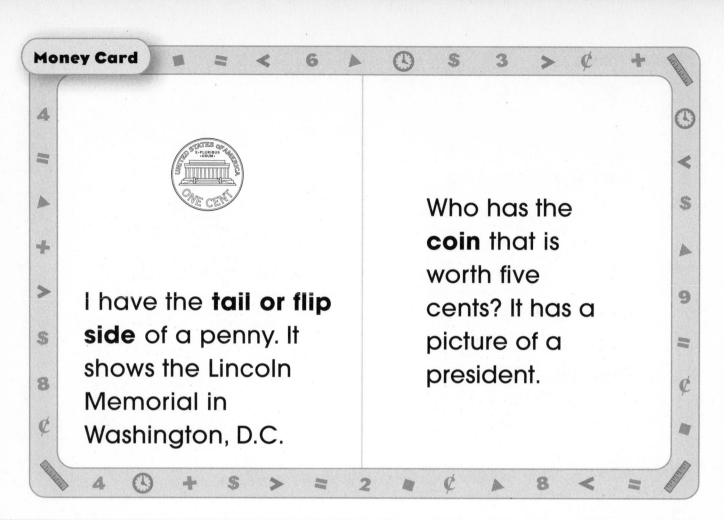

I have the **tail or flip side** of a penny. It shows the Lincoln Memorial in Washington, D.C.

Who has the **coin** that is worth five cents? It has a picture of a president.

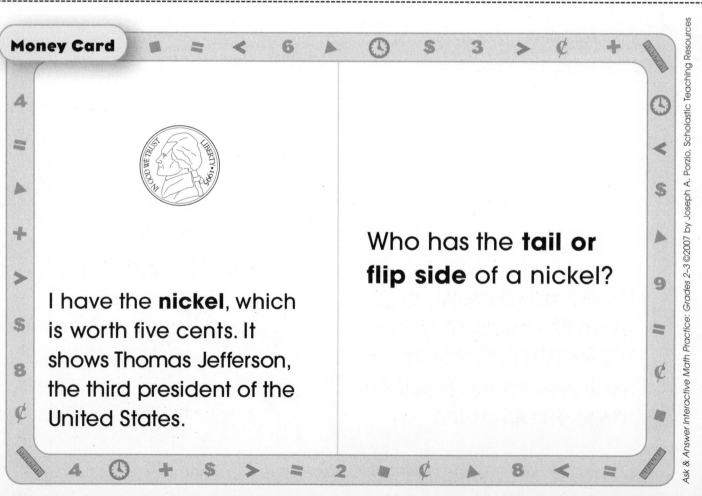

I have the **nickel**, which is worth five cents. It shows Thomas Jefferson, the third president of the United States.

Who has the **tail or flip side** of a nickel?

Ask & Answer Interactive Math Practice: Grades 2–3 ©2007 by Joseph A. Porzio, Scholastic Teaching Resources

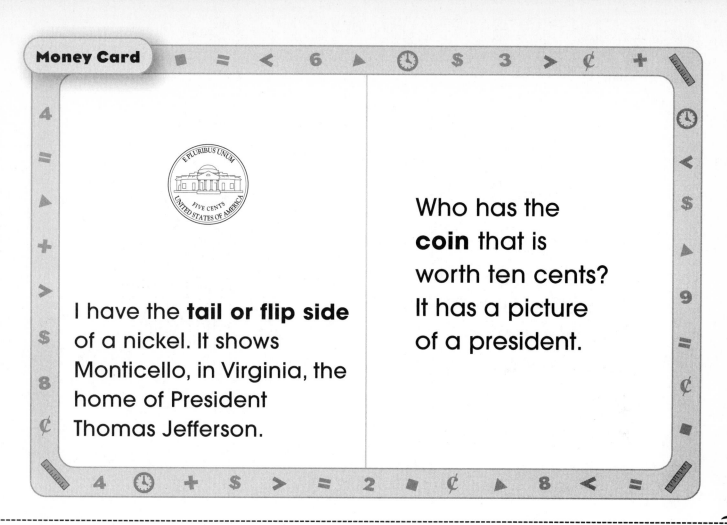

I have the **tail or flip side** of a nickel. It shows Monticello, in Virginia, the home of President Thomas Jefferson.

Who has the **coin** that is worth ten cents? It has a picture of a president.

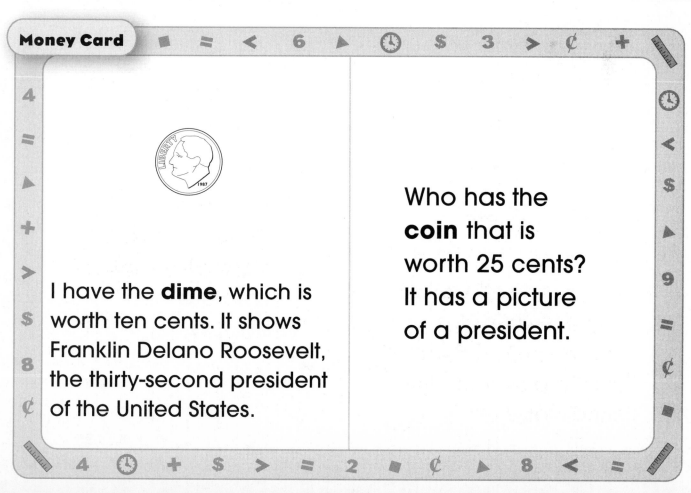

I have the **dime**, which is worth ten cents. It shows Franklin Delano Roosevelt, the thirty-second president of the United States.

Who has the **coin** that is worth 25 cents? It has a picture of a president.

Ask & Answer Interactive Math Practice: Grades 2–3 ©2007 by Joseph A. Porzio, Scholastic Teaching Resources

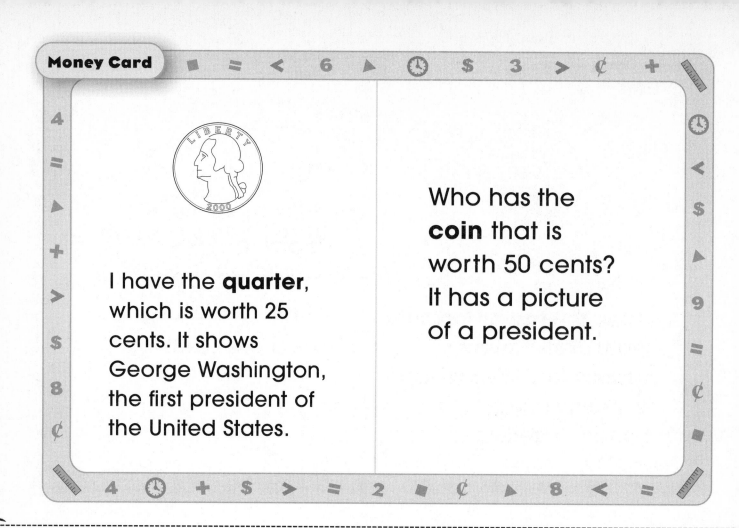

I have the **quarter**, which is worth 25 cents. It shows George Washington, the first president of the United States.

Who has the **coin** that is worth 50 cents? It has a picture of a president.

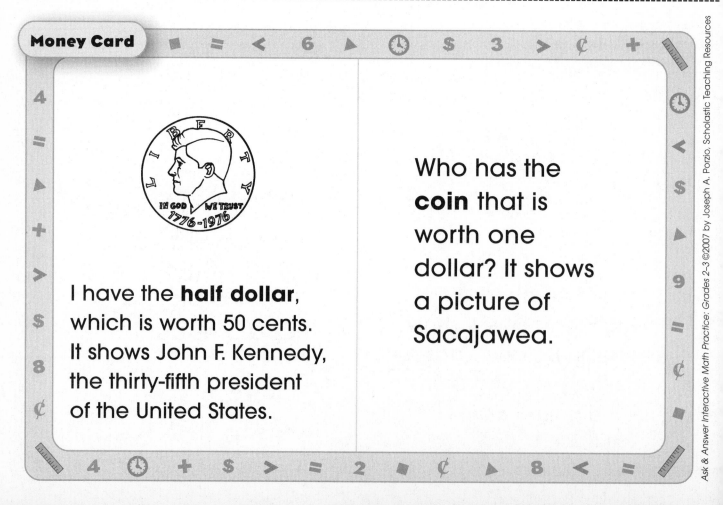

I have the **half dollar**, which is worth 50 cents. It shows John F. Kennedy, the thirty-fifth president of the United States.

Who has the **coin** that is worth one dollar? It shows a picture of Sacajawea.

Ask & Answer Interactive Math Practice: Grades 2-3 ©2007 by Joseph A. Porzio, Scholastic Teaching Resources

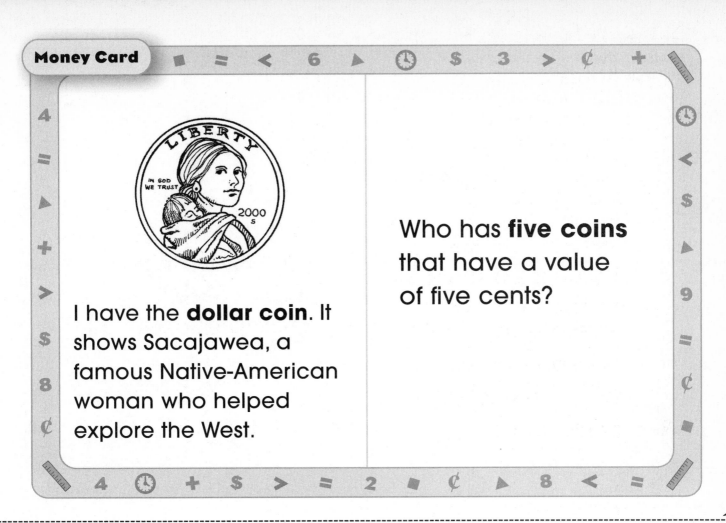

I have the **dollar coin**. It shows Sacajawea, a famous Native-American woman who helped explore the West.

Who has **five coins** that have a value of five cents?

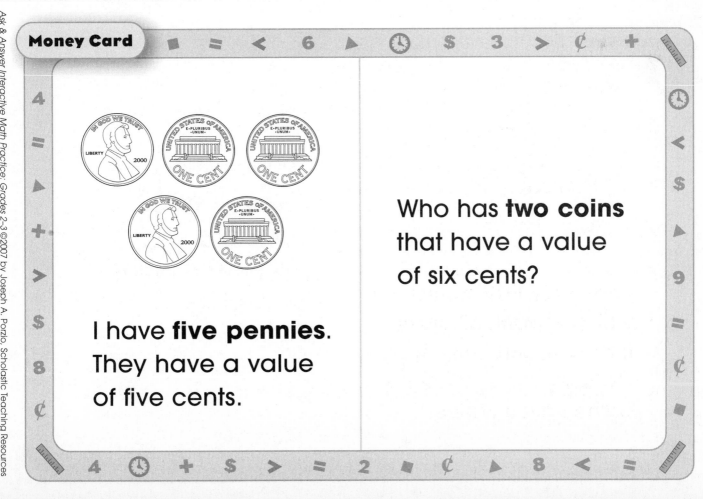

I have **five pennies**. They have a value of five cents.

Who has **two coins** that have a value of six cents?

Ask & Answer Interactive Math Practice: Grades 2–3 ©2007 by Joseph A. Porzio, Scholastic Teaching Resources

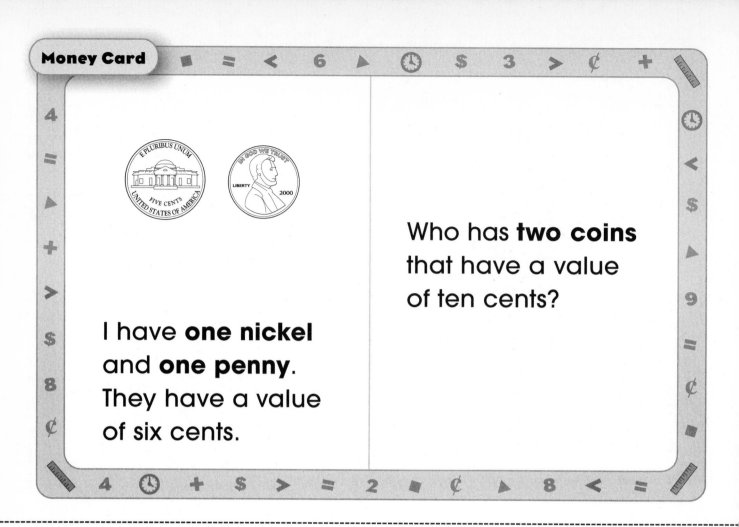

Who has **two coins** that have a value of ten cents?

I have **one nickel** and **one penny**. They have a value of six cents.

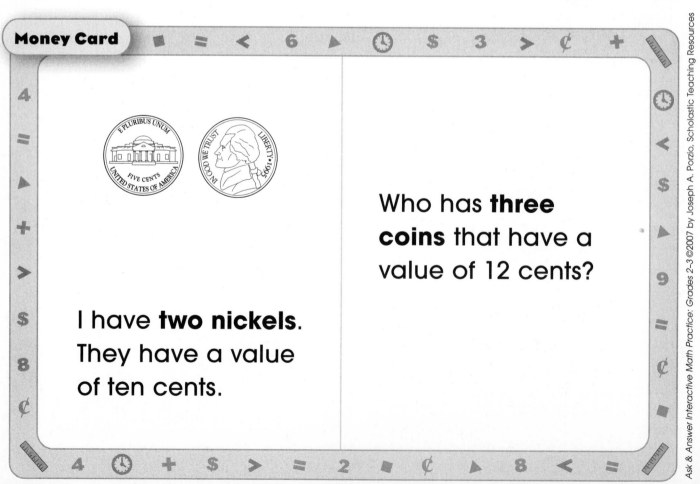

Who has **three coins** that have a value of 12 cents?

I have **two nickels**. They have a value of ten cents.

Ask & Answer Interactive Math Practice: Grades 2–3 ©2007 by Joseph A. Porzio, Scholastic Teaching Resources

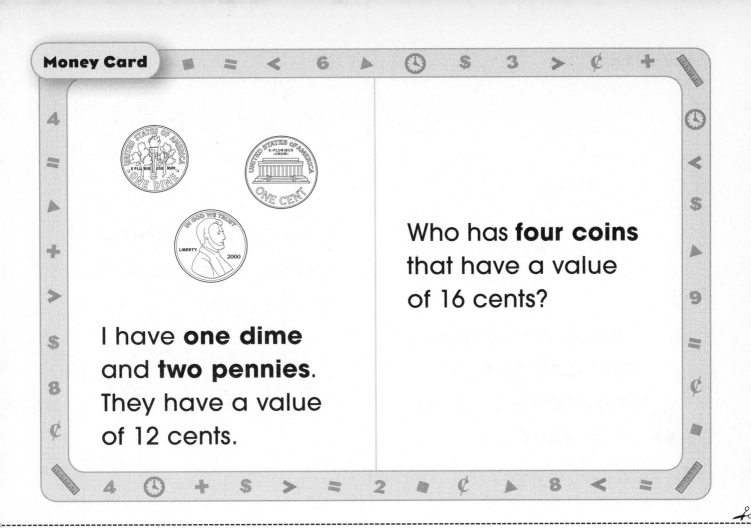

I have **one dime** and **two pennies**. They have a value of 12 cents.

Who has **four coins** that have a value of 16 cents?

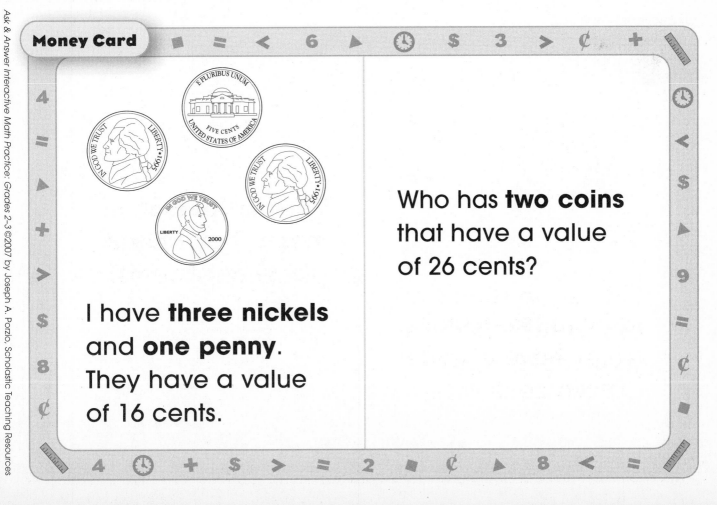

I have **three nickels** and **one penny**. They have a value of 16 cents.

Who has **two coins** that have a value of 26 cents?

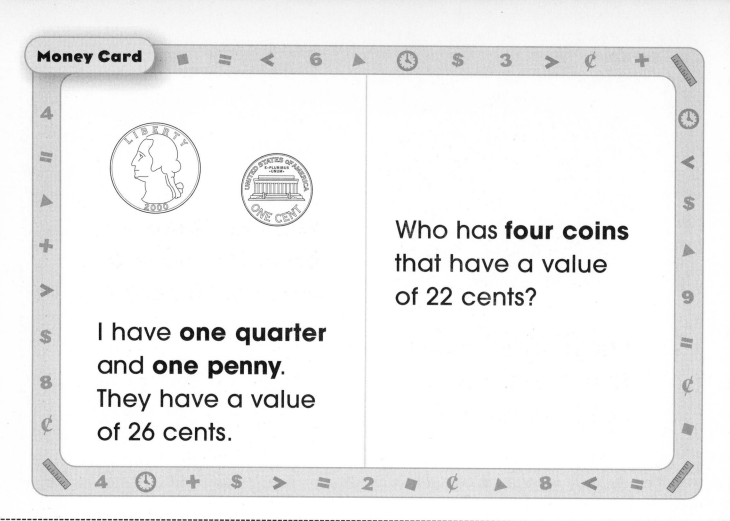

I have **one quarter** and **one penny**. They have a value of 26 cents.

Who has **four coins** that have a value of 22 cents?

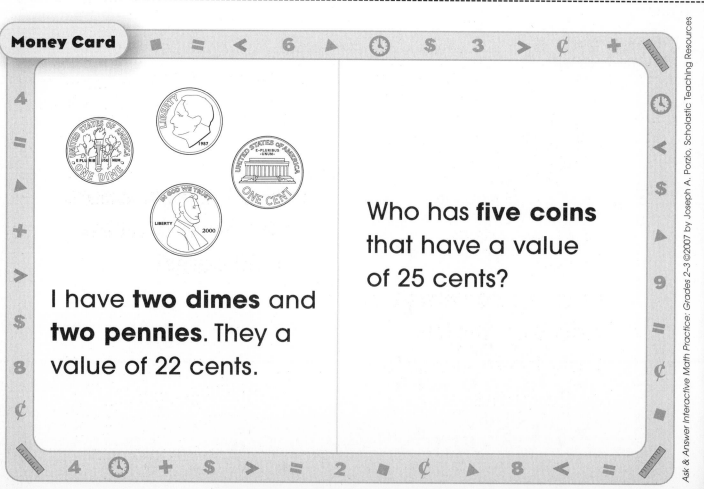

I have **two dimes** and **two pennies**. They a value of 22 cents.

Who has **five coins** that have a value of 25 cents?

Ask & Answer Interactive Math Practice: Grades 2–3 ©2007 by Joseph A. Porzio, Scholastic Teaching Resources

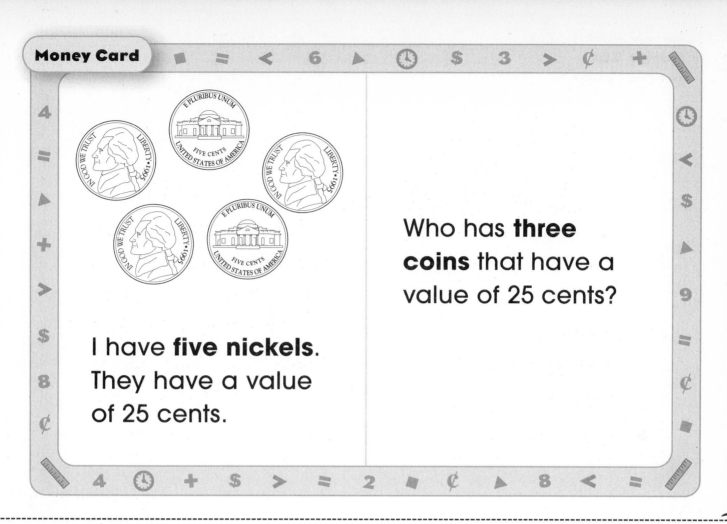

I have **five nickels**. They have a value of 25 cents.

Who has **three coins** that have a value of 25 cents?

Money Card

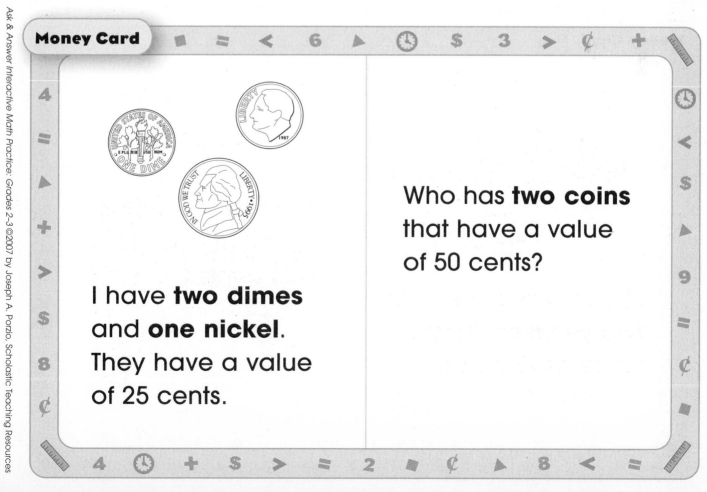

I have **two dimes** and **one nickel**. They have a value of 25 cents.

Who has **two coins** that have a value of 50 cents?

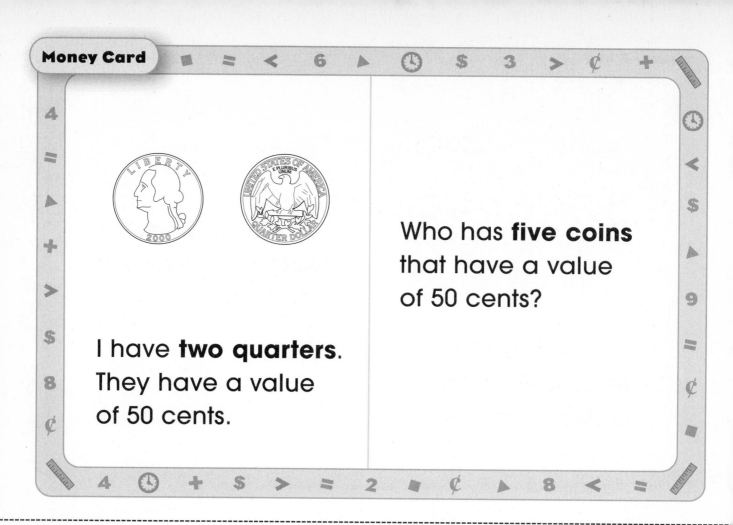

Who has **five coins** that have a value of 50 cents?

I have **two quarters**. They have a value of 50 cents.

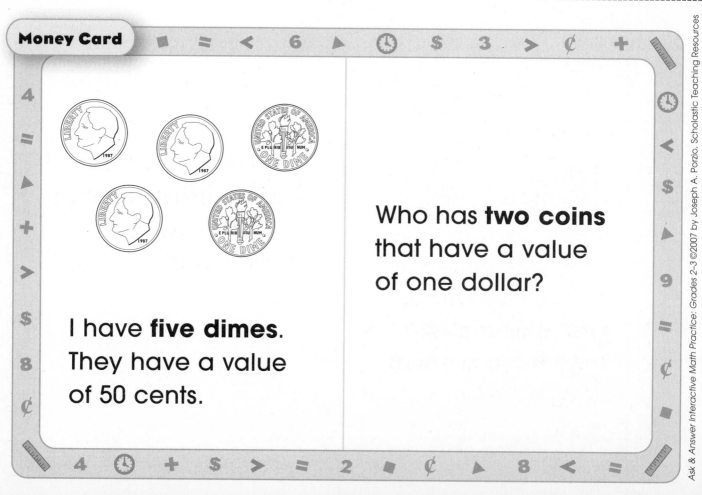

Who has **two coins** that have a value of one dollar?

I have **five dimes**. They have a value of 50 cents.

Ask & Answer Interactive Math Practice: Grades 2–3 ©2007 by Joseph A. Porzio, Scholastic Teaching Resources

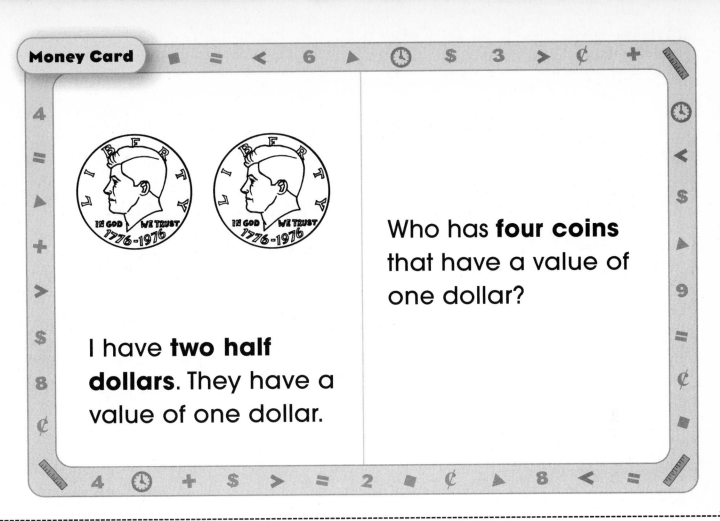

I have **two half dollars**. They have a value of one dollar.

Who has **four coins** that have a value of one dollar?

Ask & Answer Interactive Math Practice: Grades 2–3 ©2007 by Joseph A. Porzio, Scholastic Teaching Resources

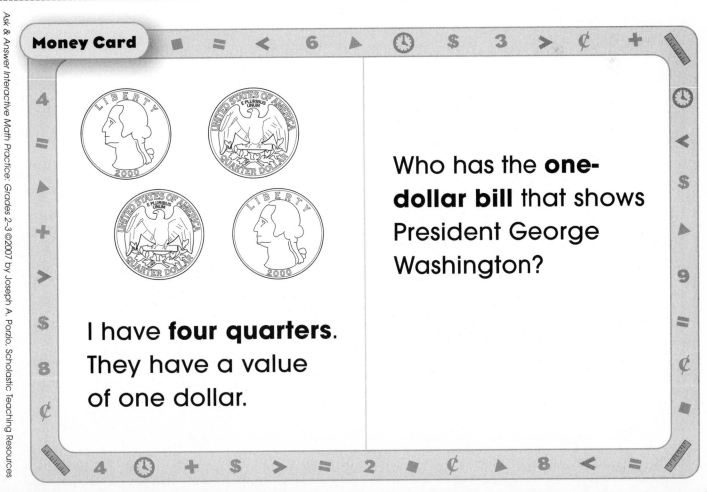

I have **four quarters**. They have a value of one dollar.

Who has the **one-dollar bill** that shows President George Washington?

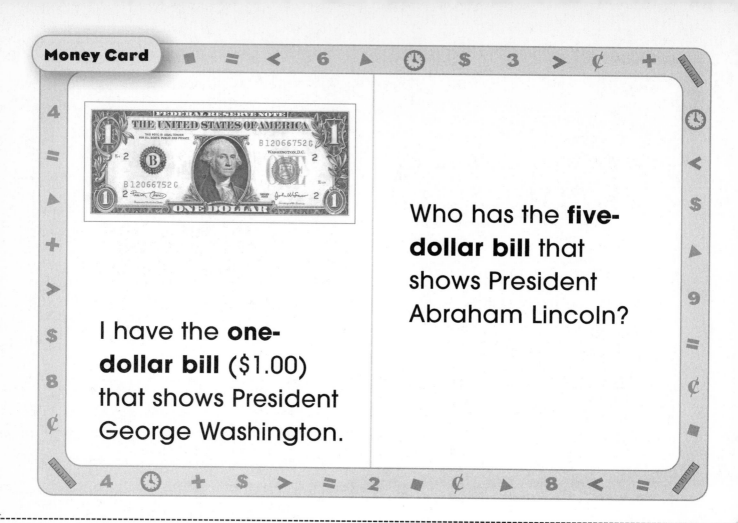

I have the **one-dollar bill** ($1.00) that shows President George Washington.

Who has the **five-dollar bill** that shows President Abraham Lincoln?

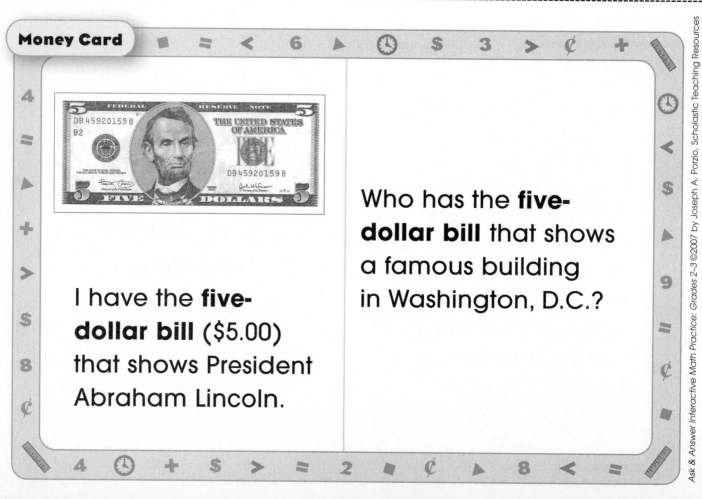

I have the **five-dollar bill** ($5.00) that shows President Abraham Lincoln.

Who has the **five-dollar bill** that shows a famous building in Washington, D.C.?

Ask & Answer Interactive Math Practice: Grades 2–3 ©2007 by Joseph A. Porzio, Scholastic Teaching Resources

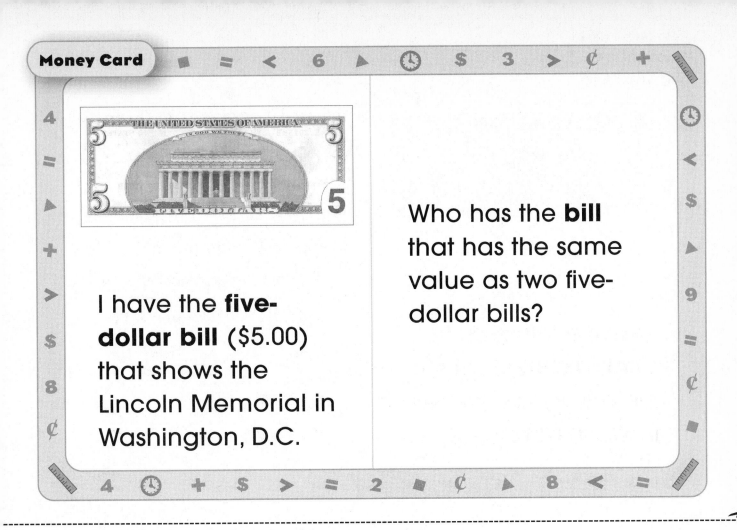

I have the **five-dollar bill** ($5.00) that shows the Lincoln Memorial in Washington, D.C.

Who has the **bill** that has the same value as two five-dollar bills?

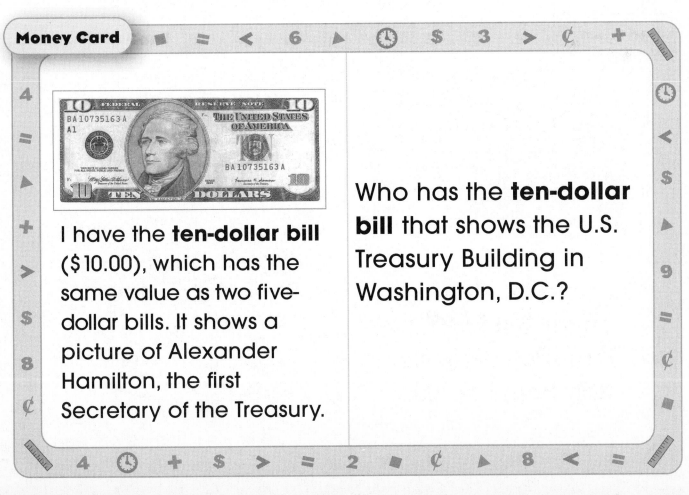

I have the **ten-dollar bill** ($10.00), which has the same value as two five-dollar bills. It shows a picture of Alexander Hamilton, the first Secretary of the Treasury.

Who has the **ten-dollar bill** that shows the U.S. Treasury Building in Washington, D.C.?

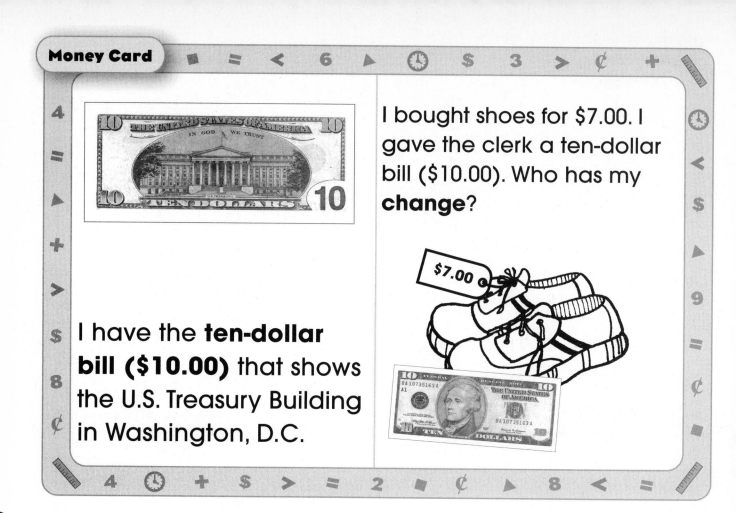

I bought shoes for $7.00. I gave the clerk a ten-dollar bill ($10.00). Who has my **change**?

$7.00

I have the **ten-dollar bill ($10.00)** that shows the U.S. Treasury Building in Washington, D.C.

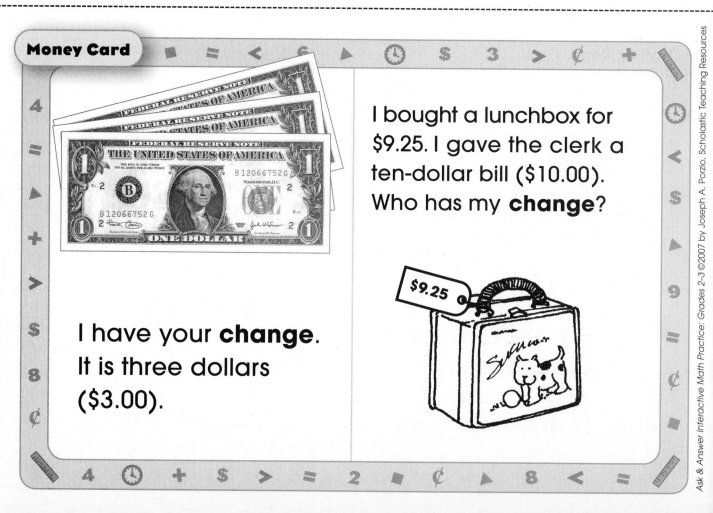

I bought a lunchbox for $9.25. I gave the clerk a ten-dollar bill ($10.00). Who has my **change**?

$9.25

I have your **change**. It is three dollars ($3.00).

Ask & Answer Interactive Math Practice: Grades 2–3 ©2007 by Joseph A. Porzio, Scholastic Teaching Resources

I bought a book for $3.00. I gave the clerk a five-dollar bill ($5.00). Who has my **change**?

I have your **change**. It is seventy-five cents (75¢).

$3.00

Ask & Answer Interactive Math Practice: Grades 2–3 ©2007 by Joseph A. Porzio, Scholastic Teaching Resources

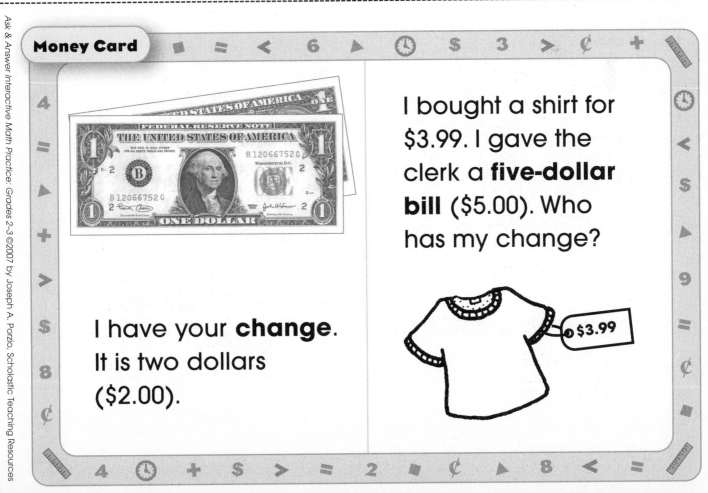

I bought a shirt for $3.99. I gave the clerk a **five-dollar bill** ($5.00). Who has my change?

I have your **change**. It is two dollars ($2.00).

$3.99

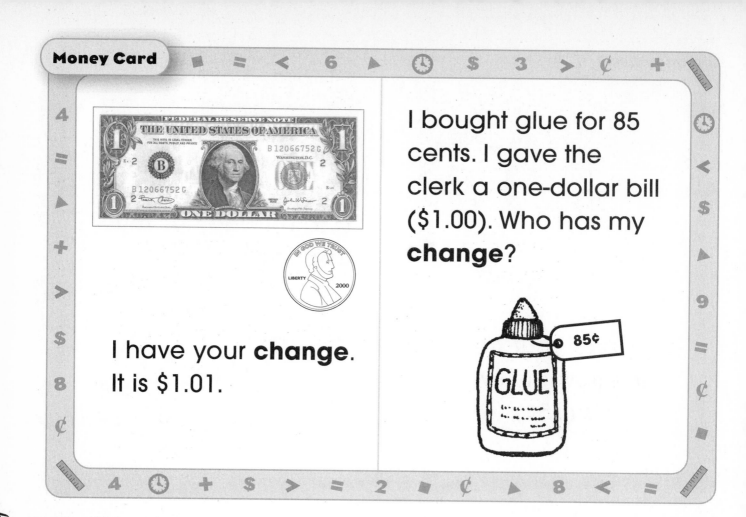

I bought glue for 85 cents. I gave the clerk a one-dollar bill ($1.00). Who has my **change**?

I have your **change**. It is $1.01.

85¢

GLUE

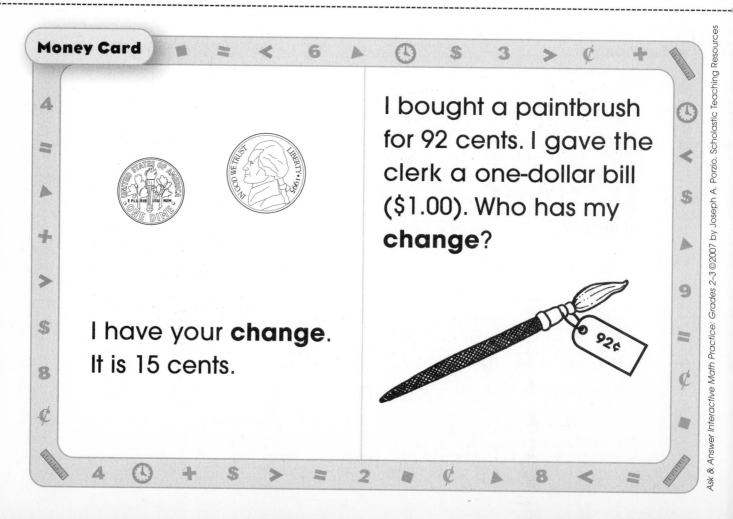

I bought a paintbrush for 92 cents. I gave the clerk a one-dollar bill ($1.00). Who has my **change**?

I have your **change**. It is 15 cents.

92¢

Ask & Answer Interactive Math Practice: Grades 2–3 ©2007 by Joseph A. Porzio, Scholastic Teaching Resources

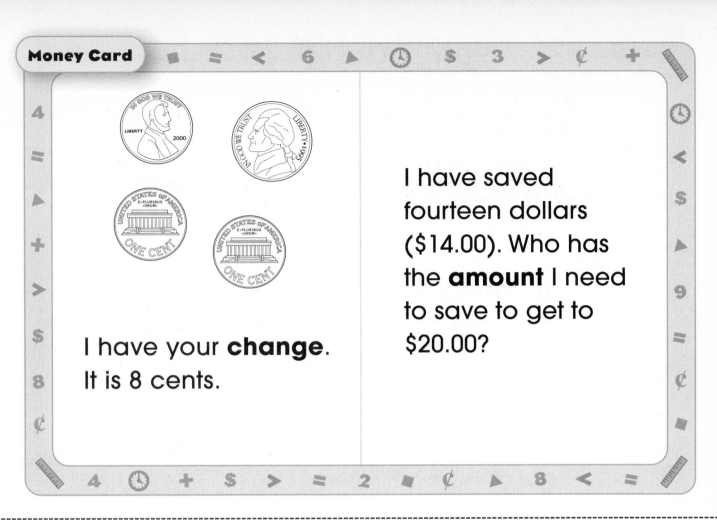

I have your **change**.
It is 8 cents.

I have saved
fourteen dollars
($14.00). Who has
the **amount** I need
to save to get to
$20.00?

Ask & Answer Interactive Math Practice: Grades 2–3 ©2007 by Joseph A. Porzio, Scholastic Teaching Resources

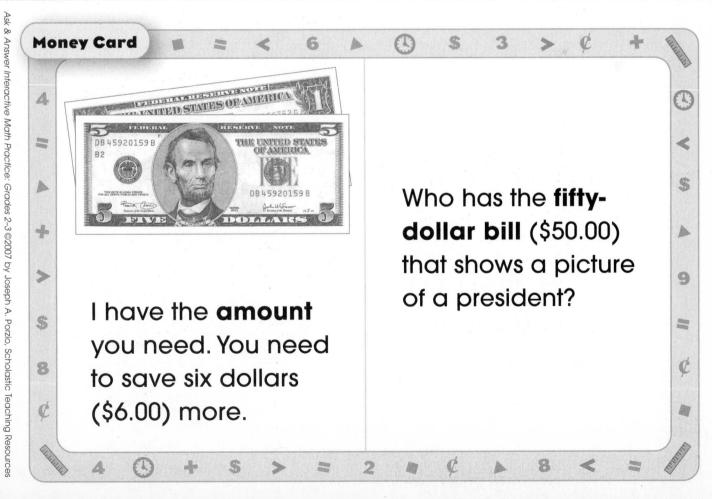

I have the **amount**
you need. You need
to save six dollars
($6.00) more.

Who has the **fifty-dollar bill** ($50.00)
that shows a picture
of a president?

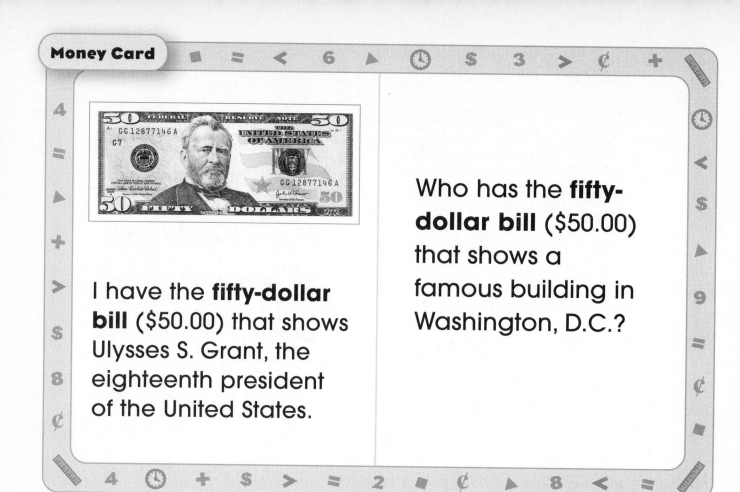

I have the **fifty-dollar bill** ($50.00) that shows Ulysses S. Grant, the eighteenth president of the United States.

Who has the **fifty-dollar bill** ($50.00) that shows a famous building in Washington, D.C.?

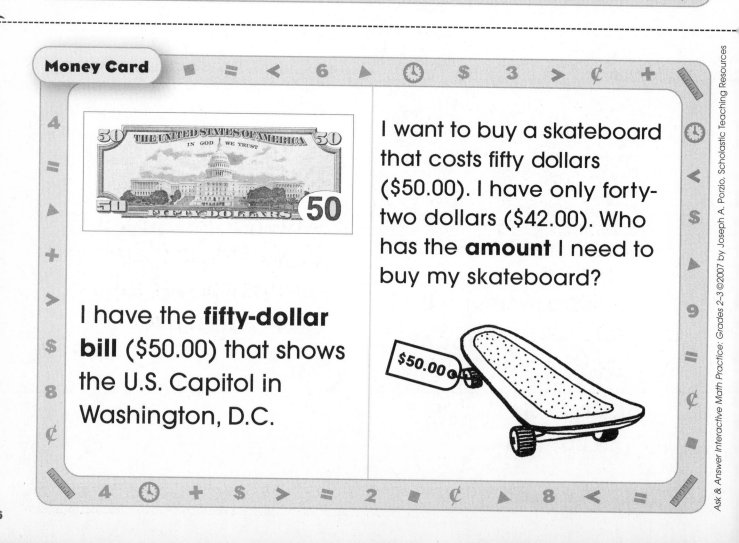

I have the **fifty-dollar bill** ($50.00) that shows the U.S. Capitol in Washington, D.C.

I want to buy a skateboard that costs fifty dollars ($50.00). I have only forty-two dollars ($42.00). Who has the **amount** I need to buy my skateboard?

$50.00

Ask & Answer Interactive Math Practice: Grades 2–3 ©2007 by Joseph A. Porzio, Scholastic Teaching Resources

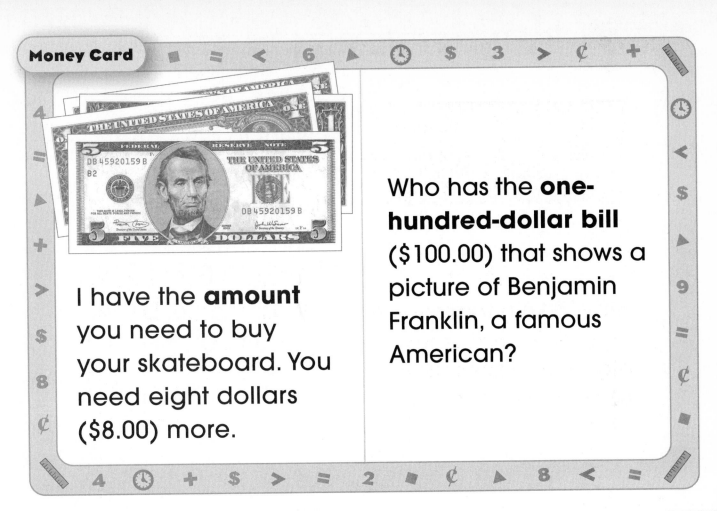

I have the **amount** you need to buy your skateboard. You need eight dollars ($8.00) more.

Who has the **one-hundred-dollar bill** ($100.00) that shows a picture of Benjamin Franklin, a famous American?

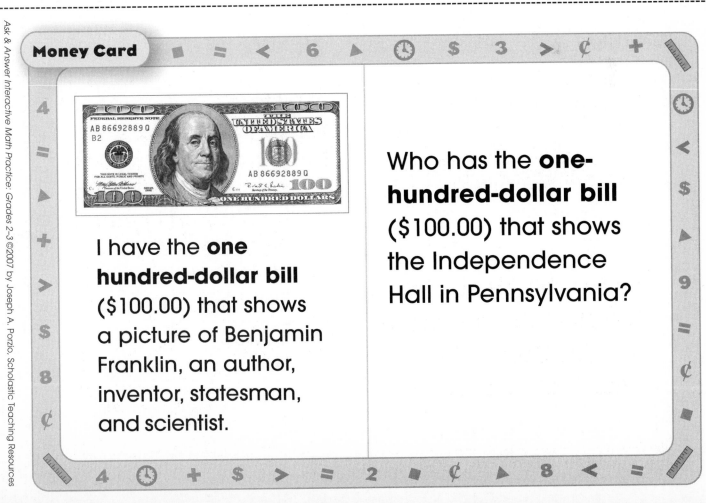

I have the **one hundred-dollar bill** ($100.00) that shows a picture of Benjamin Franklin, an author, inventor, statesman, and scientist.

Who has the **one-hundred-dollar bill** ($100.00) that shows the Independence Hall in Pennsylvania?

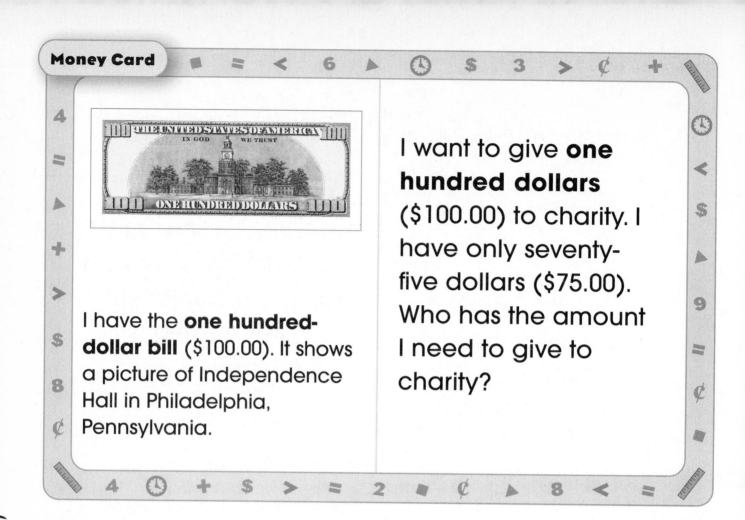

I have the **one hundred-dollar bill** ($100.00). It shows a picture of Independence Hall in Philadelphia, Pennsylvania.

I want to give **one hundred dollars** ($100.00) to charity. I have only seventy-five dollars ($75.00). Who has the amount I need to give to charity?

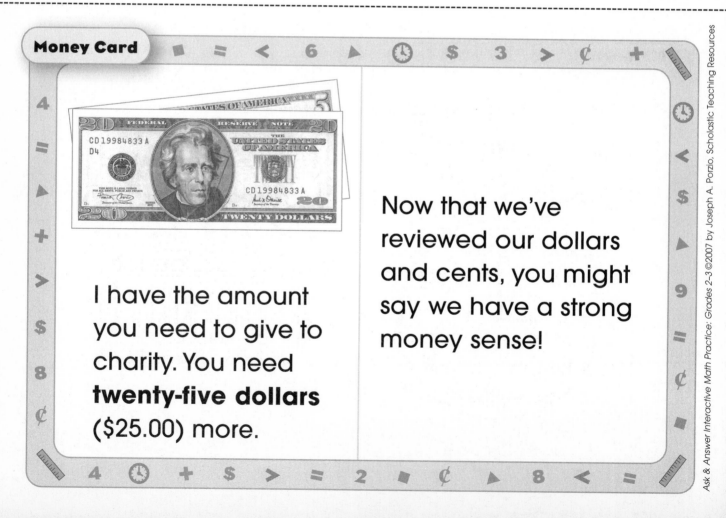

I have the amount you need to give to charity. You need **twenty-five dollars** ($25.00) more.

Now that we've reviewed our dollars and cents, you might say we have a strong money sense!

Ask & Answer Interactive Math Practice: Grades 2–3 ©2007 by Joseph A. Porzio, Scholastic Teaching Resources

I have a "happy face" clock ready to start the game.

Who has…?

I have….

Who has…?

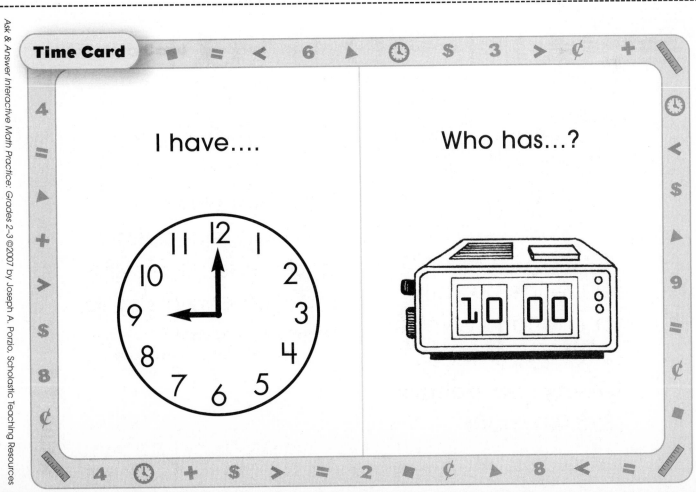

I have....

Who has...?

I have....

Who has...?

Ask & Answer Interactive Math Practice: Grades 2–3 © 2007 by Joseph A. Porzio, Scholastic Teaching Resources

I have....

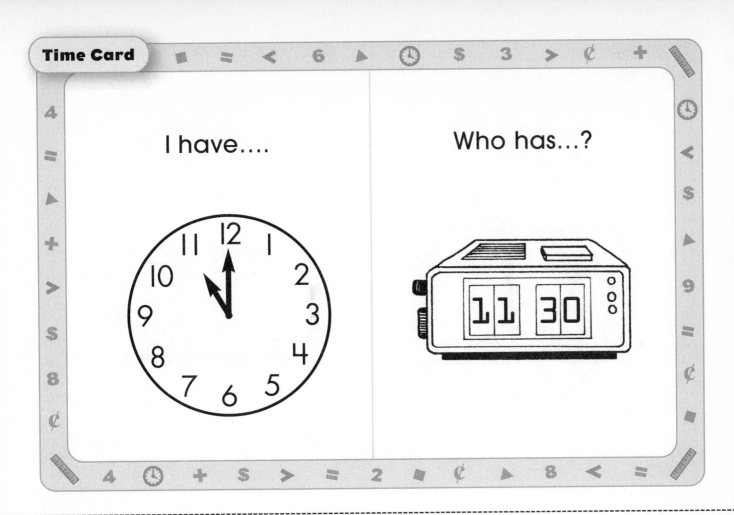

Who has...?

I have....

Who has...?

I have....

Who has...?

I have....

Who has...?

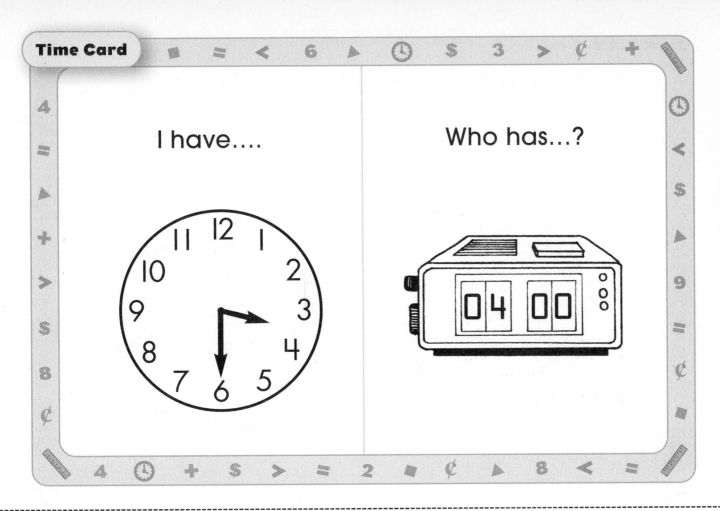

I have....

Who has...?

Ask & Answer Interactive Math Practice: Grades 2–3 © 2007 by Joseph A. Porzio, Scholastic Teaching Resources

I have....

Who has...?

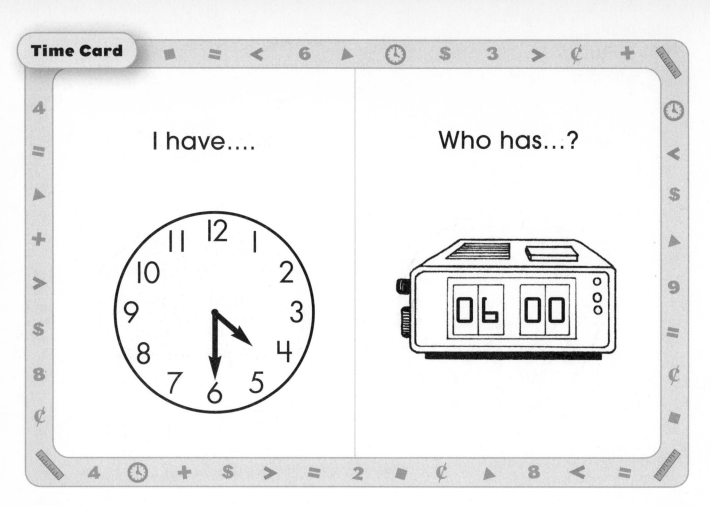

Time Card

I have....

Who has...?

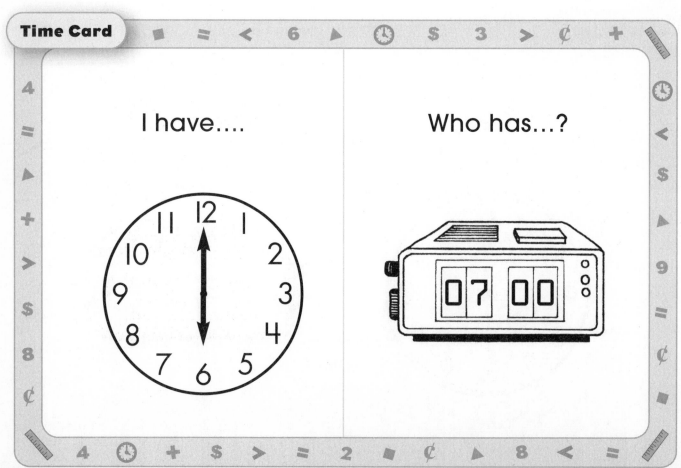

Time Card

I have....

Who has...?

Ask & Answer Interactive Math Practice: Grades 2–3 © 2007 by Joseph A. Porzio, Scholastic Teaching Resources

Ask & Answer Interactive Math Practice: Grades 2–3 © 2007 by Joseph A. Porzio. Scholastic Teaching Resources

Time Card

I have....

Who has...?

Time Card

I have....

Who has...?

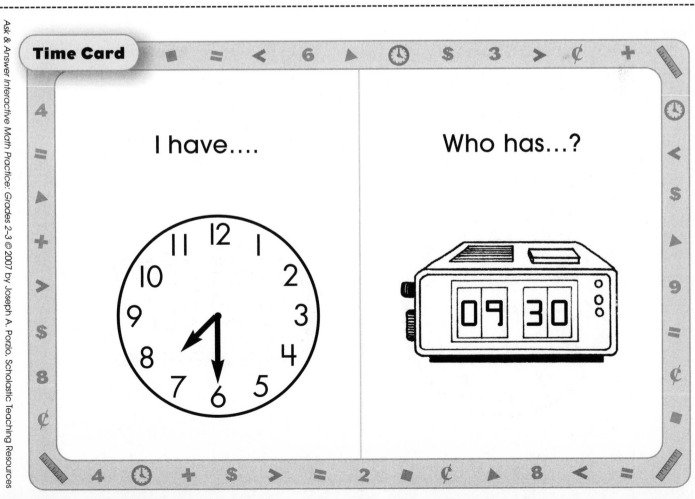

I have....

Who has...?

I have....

Who has...?

I have....

Who has...?

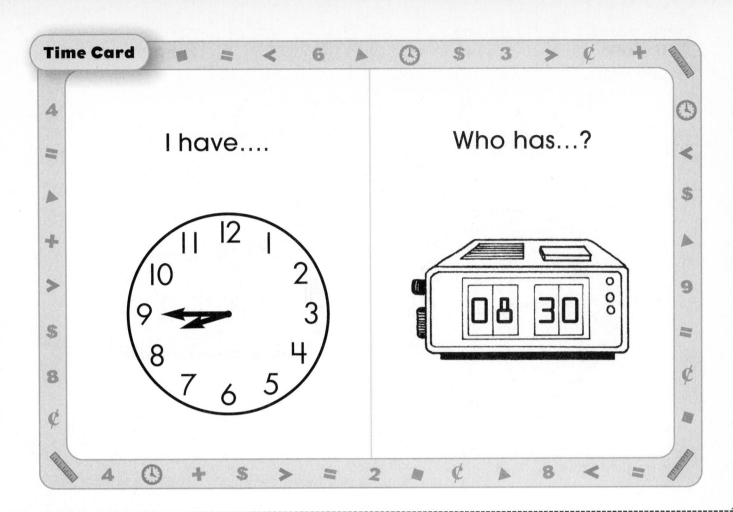

I have....

Who has...?

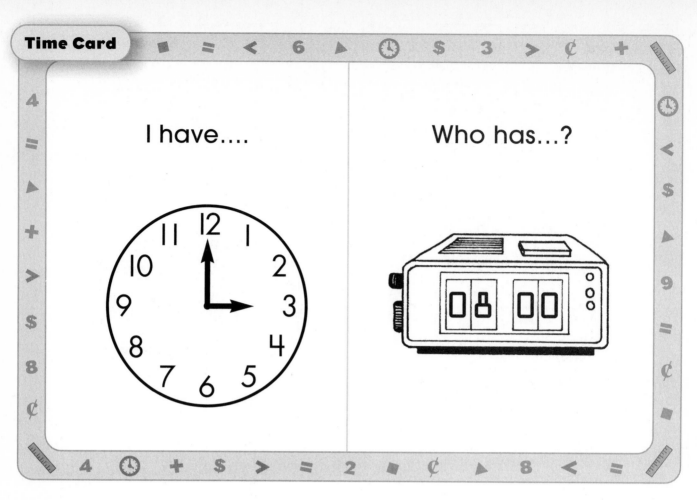

Time Card

I have....

Who has...?

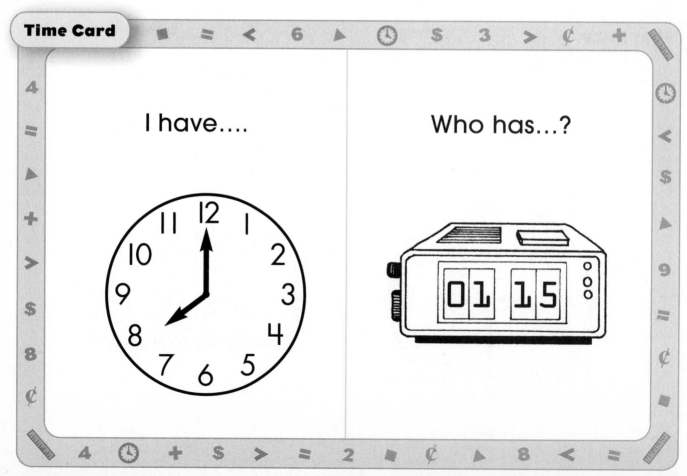

Time Card

I have....

Who has...?

Ask & Answer Interactive Math Practice: Grades 2–3 © 2007 by Joseph A. Porzio, Scholastic Teaching Resources

I have....

Who has...?

I have....

Who has...?

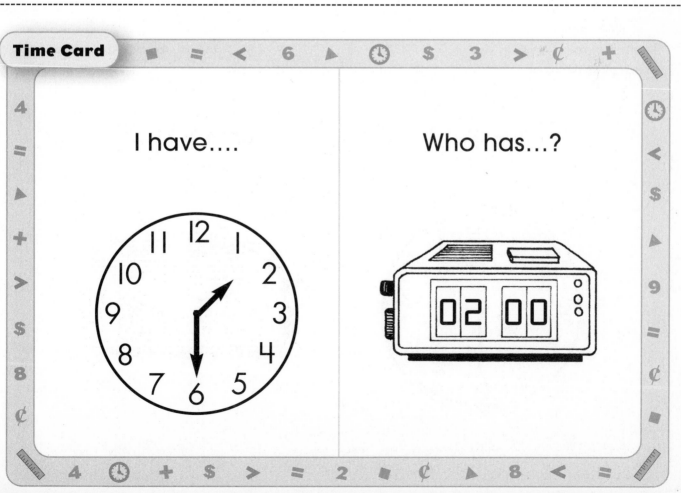

I have....

Who has...?

I have....

Who has...?

Ask & Answer Interactive Math Practice: Grades 2–3 © 2007 by Joseph A. Porzio, Scholastic Teaching Resources

I have....

Who has...?

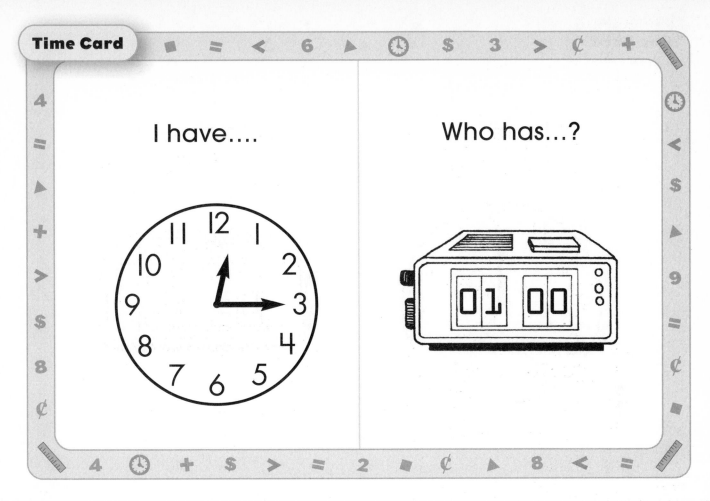

I have....

Who has...?

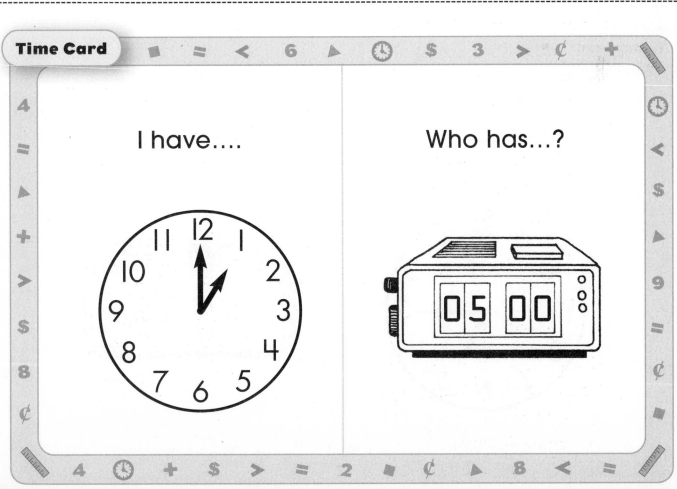

I have....

Who has...?

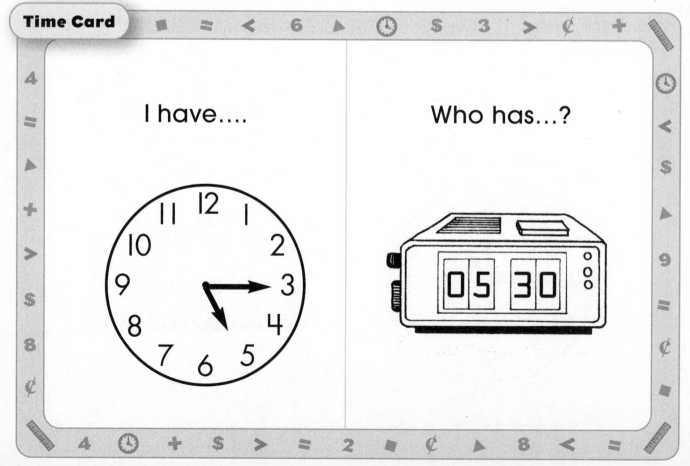

I have....

Who has...?

Time Card

I have....

Who has...?

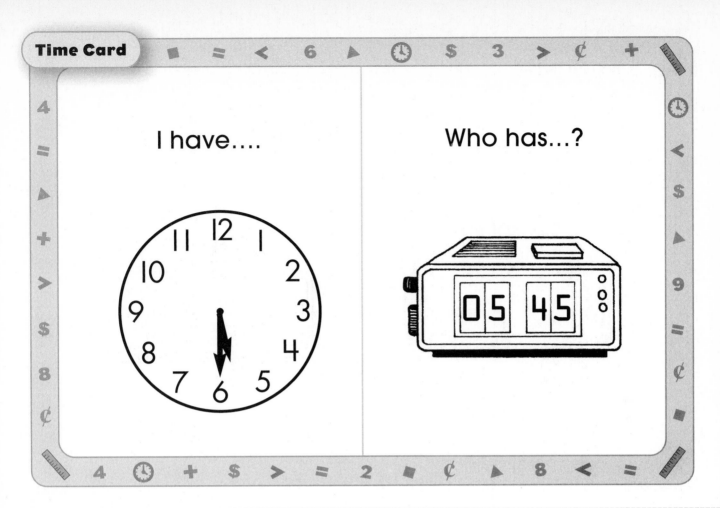

Time Card

I have....

Who has...?

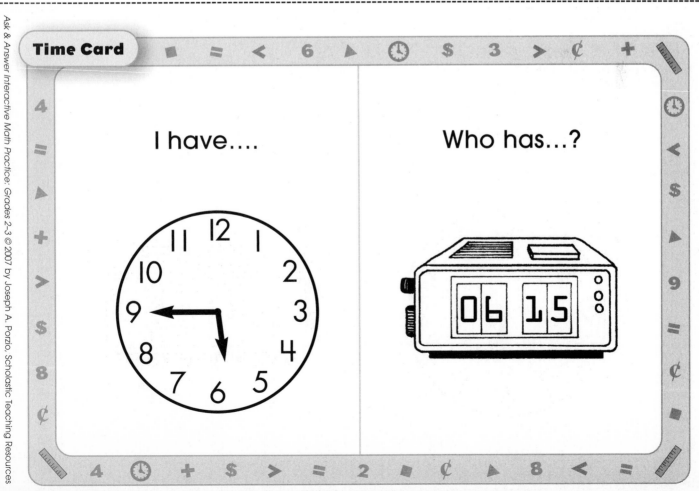

I have....

Who has...?

06 30

I have....

Who has...?

06 45

Ask & Answer Interactive Math Practice: Grades 2–3 © 2007 by Joseph A. Porzio, Scholastic Teaching Resources

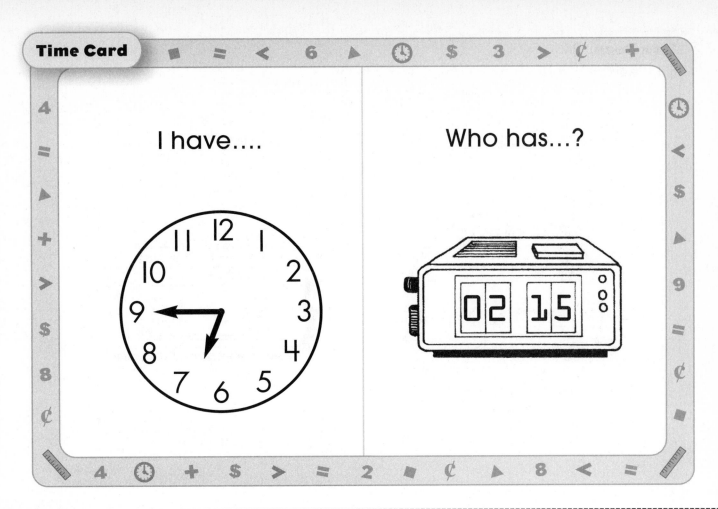

I have....

Who has...?

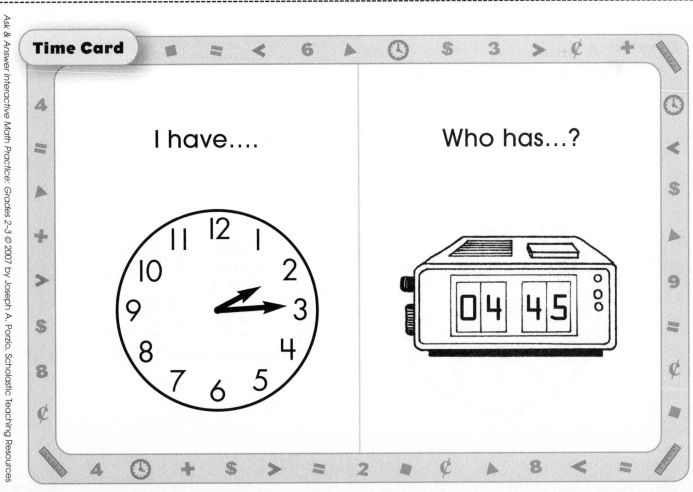

I have....

Who has...?

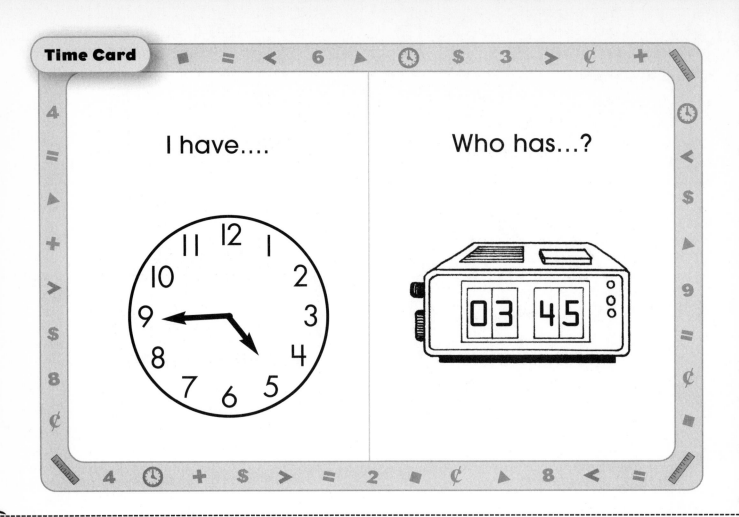

I have....

Who has...?

I have....

Who has...?

Ask & Answer Interactive Math Practice: Grades 2–3 © 2007 by Joseph A. Porzio, Scholastic Teaching Resources

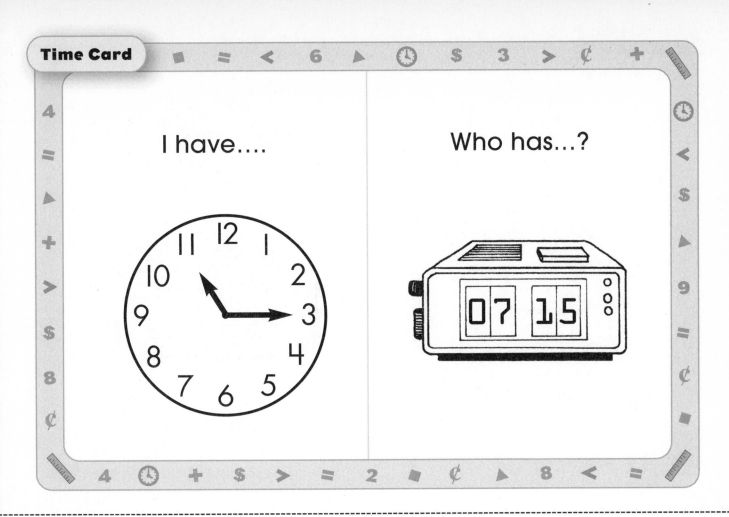

I have....   Who has...?

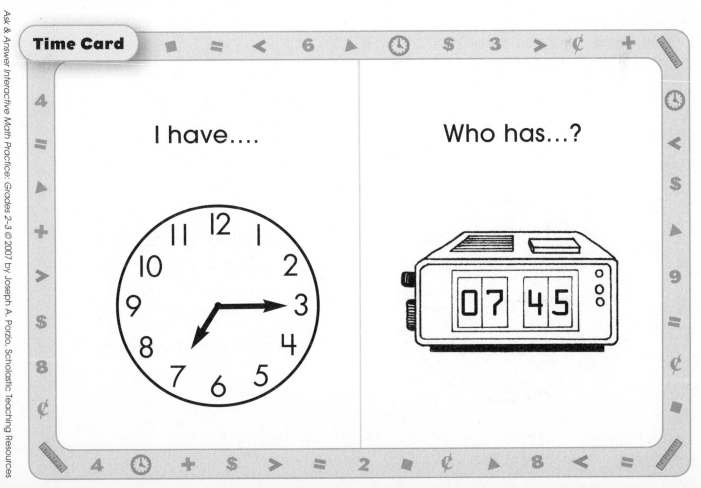

I have....   Who has...?

Ask & Answer Interactive Math Practice: Grades 2–3 © 2007 by Joseph A. Porzio, Scholastic Teaching Resources

I have....

Who has...?

I have....

And now we're out of time!

We use tools to measure every day—a ruler, a thermometer, a clock for the time of day.

Tools of measurement are things we use at school, at home, at work, and even at play.

Who has the picture of a **scale** that shows how much things weigh?

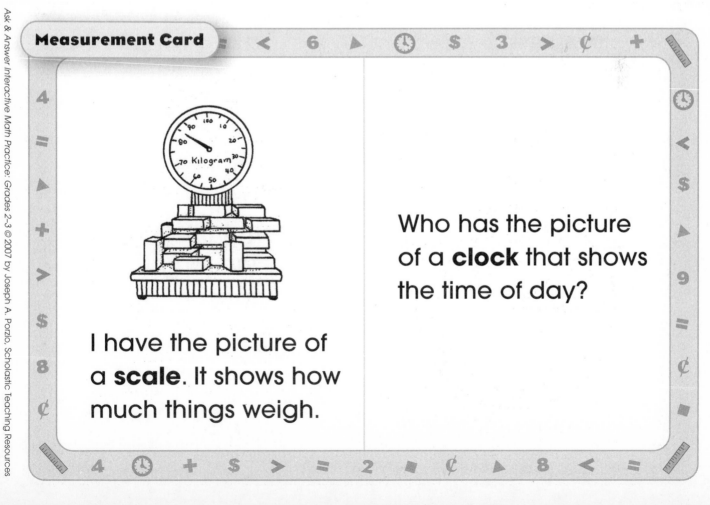

I have the picture of a **scale**. It shows how much things weigh.

Who has the picture of a **clock** that shows the time of day?

Ask & Answer Interactive Math Practice: Grades 2–3 © 2007 by Joseph A. Porzio, Scholastic Teaching Resources

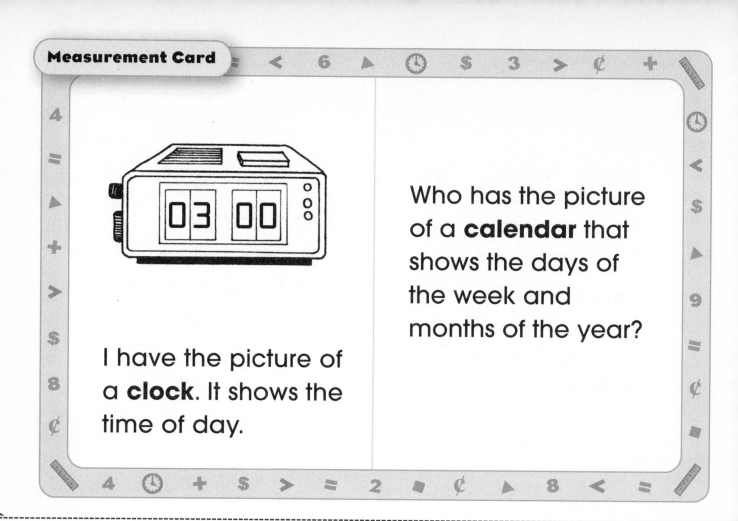

I have the picture of a **clock**. It shows the time of day.

Who has the picture of a **calendar** that shows the days of the week and months of the year?

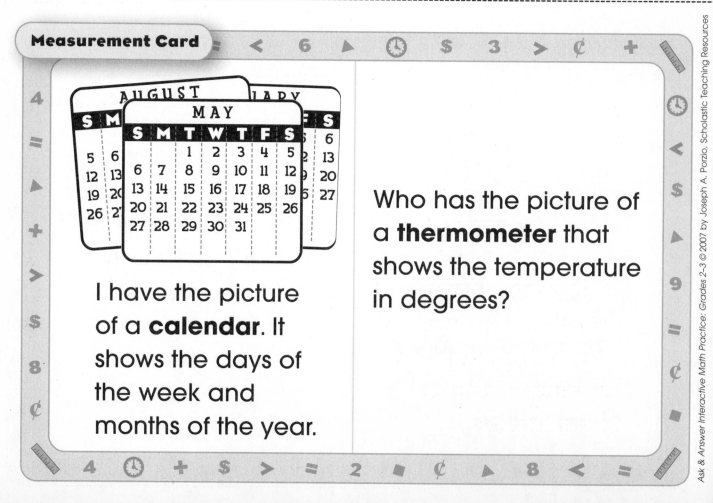

I have the picture of a **calendar**. It shows the days of the week and months of the year.

Who has the picture of a **thermometer** that shows the temperature in degrees?

Ask & Answer Interactive Math Practice: Grades 2–3 © 2007 by Joseph A. Porzio, Scholastic Teaching Resources

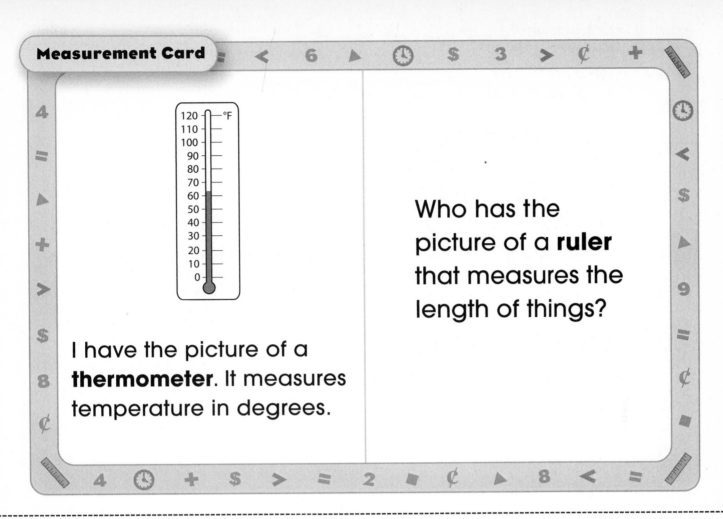

Measurement Card

I have the picture of a **thermometer**. It measures temperature in degrees.

Who has the picture of a **ruler** that measures the length of things?

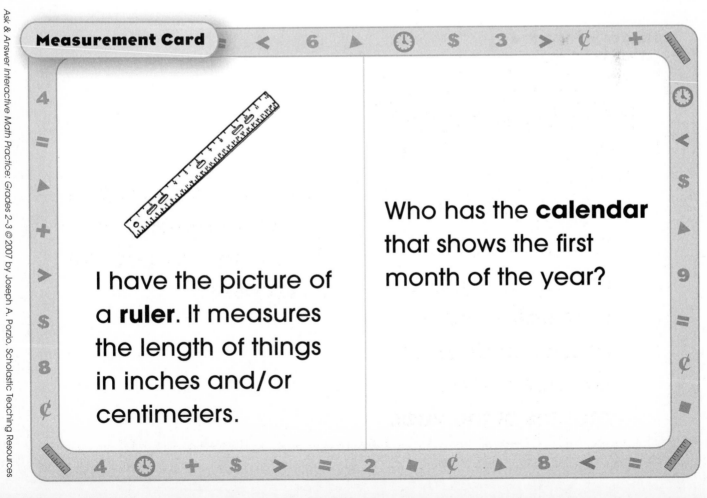

Measurement Card

I have the picture of a **ruler**. It measures the length of things in inches and/or centimeters.

Who has the **calendar** that shows the first month of the year?

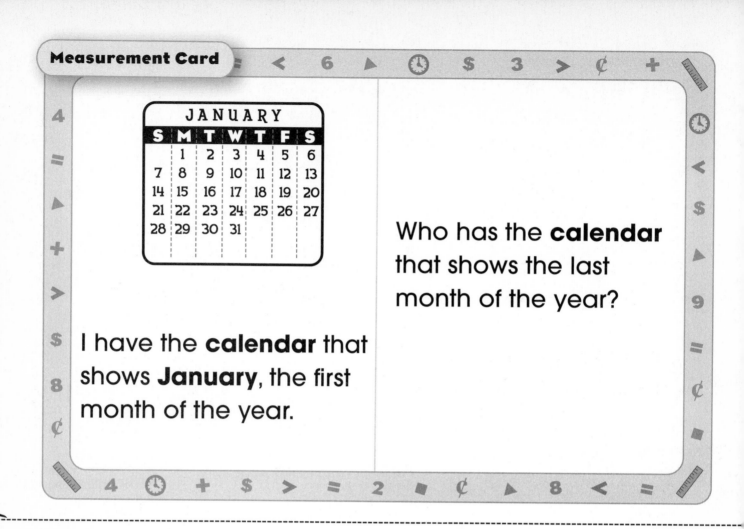

I have the **calendar** that shows **January**, the first month of the year.

Who has the **calendar** that shows the last month of the year?

I have the **calendar** that shows **December,** the last month of the year.

Who has **words** that tell about the start of a new day?

Ask & Answer Interactive Math Practice: Grades 2–3 © 2007 by Joseph A. Porzio, Scholastic Teaching Resources

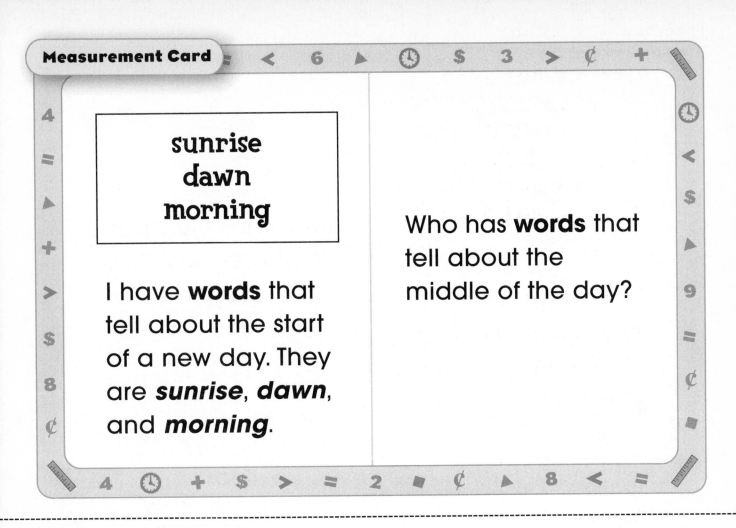

sunrise
dawn
morning

I have **words** that tell about the start of a new day. They are *sunrise*, *dawn*, and *morning*.

Who has **words** that tell about the middle of the day?

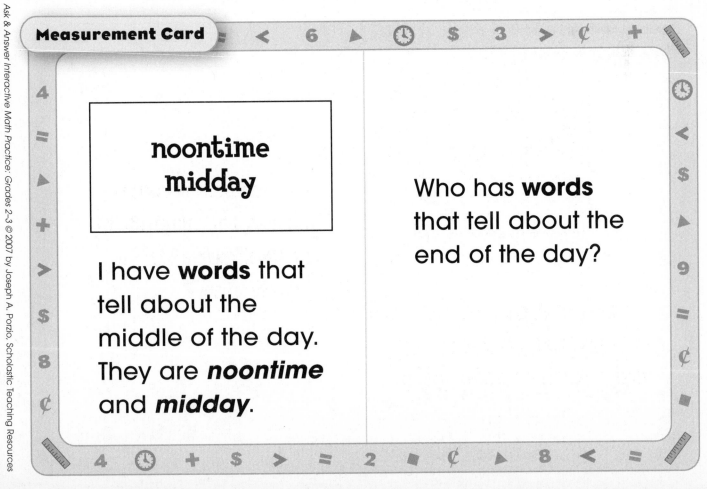

noontime
midday

I have **words** that tell about the middle of the day. They are *noontime* and *midday*.

Who has **words** that tell about the end of the day?

Ask & Answer Interactive Math Practice: Grades 2–3 © 2007 by Joseph A. Porzio, Scholastic Teaching Resources

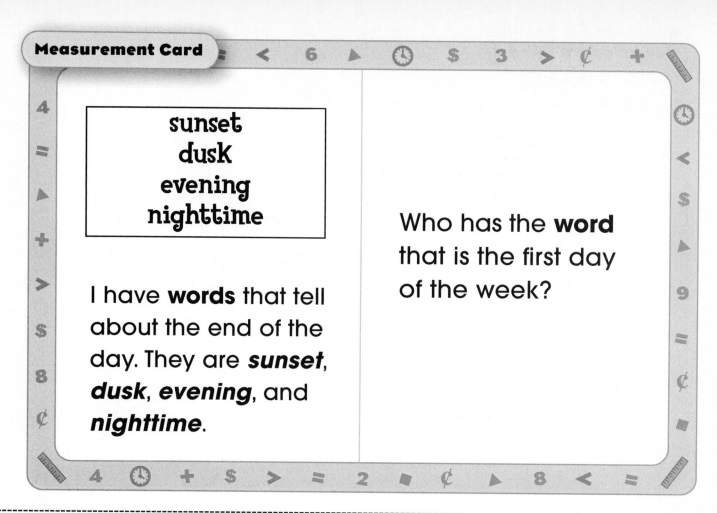

sunset
dusk
evening
nighttime

I have **words** that tell about the end of the day. They are *sunset*, *dusk*, *evening*, and *nighttime*.

Who has the **word** that is the first day of the week?

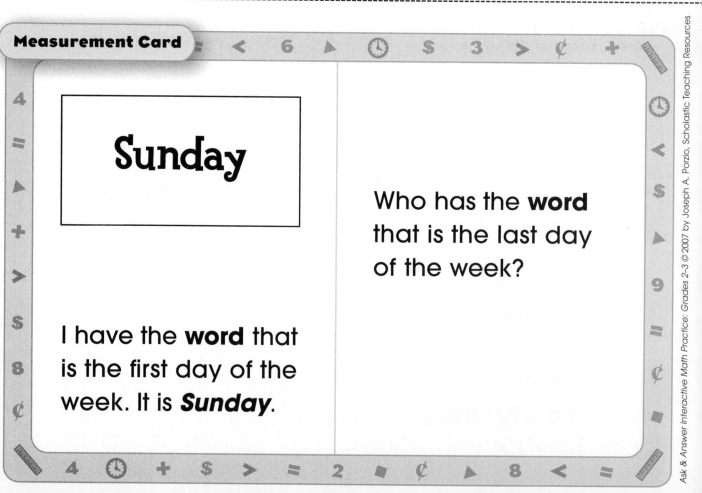

Measurement Card

Sunday

Who has the **word** that is the last day of the week?

I have the **word** that is the first day of the week. It is *Sunday*.

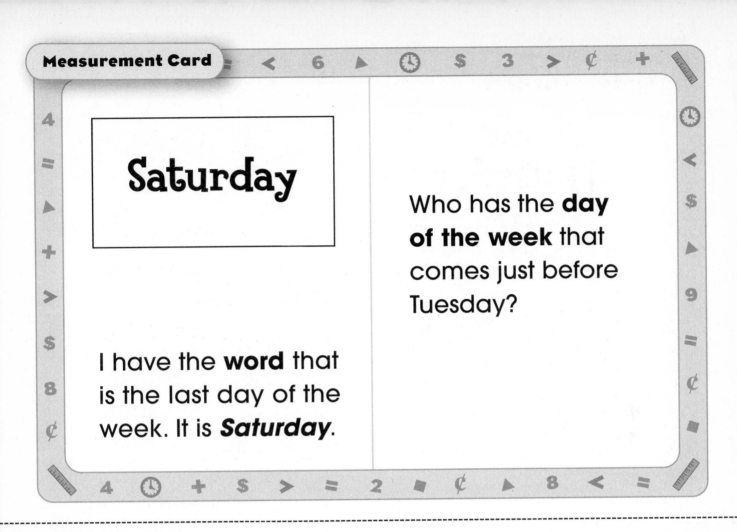

Saturday

I have the **word** that is the last day of the week. It is **Saturday**.

Who has the **day of the week** that comes just before Tuesday?

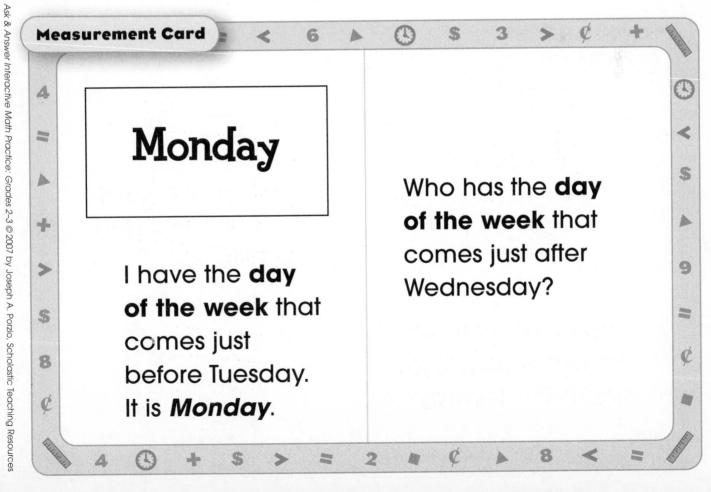

Monday

I have the **day of the week** that comes just before Tuesday. It is **Monday**.

Who has the **day of the week** that comes just after Wednesday?

Thursday

I have the **day of the week** that comes just after Wednesday. It is *Thursday*.

Who has the picture of a **glass** that is full?

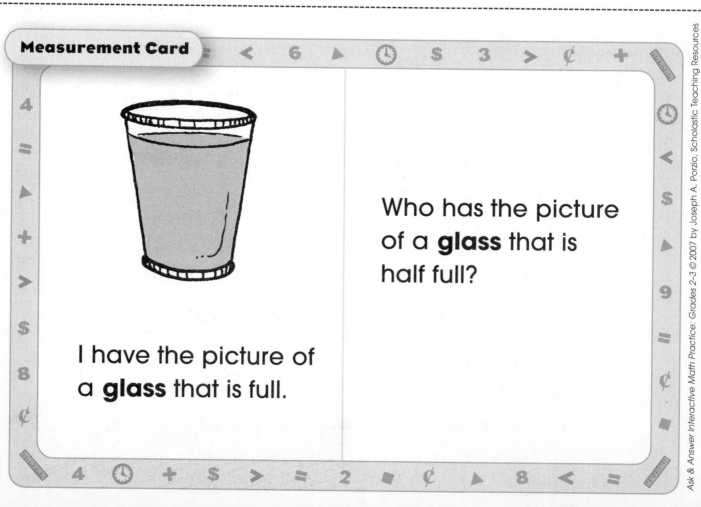

I have the picture of a **glass** that is full.

Who has the picture of a **glass** that is half full?

Ask & Answer Interactive Math Practice: Grades 2–3 © 2007 by Joseph A. Porzio, Scholastic Teaching Resources

Measurement Card

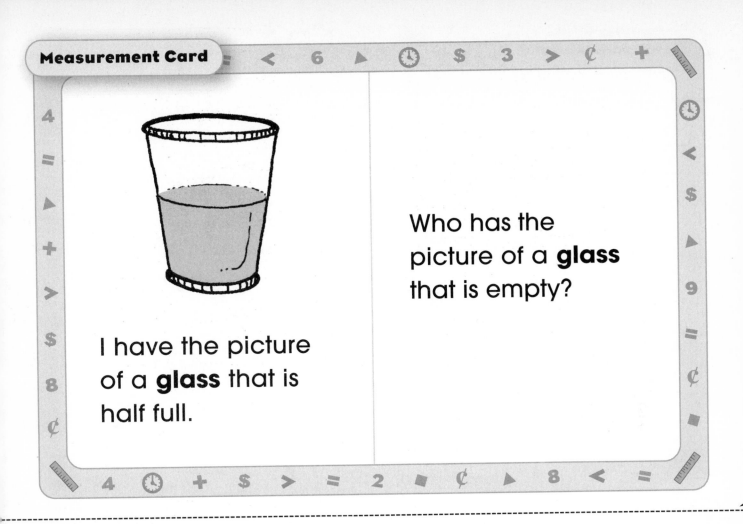

I have the picture of a **glass** that is half full.

Who has the picture of a **glass** that is empty?

Measurement Card

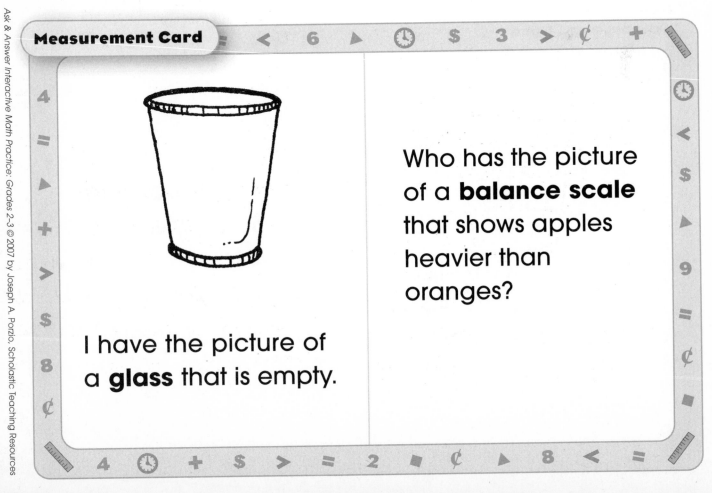

I have the picture of a **glass** that is empty.

Who has the picture of a **balance scale** that shows apples heavier than oranges?

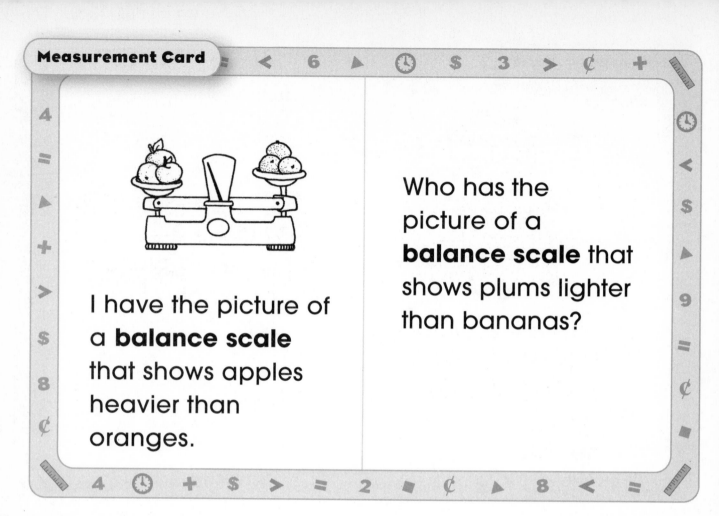

I have the picture of a **balance scale** that shows apples heavier than oranges.

Who has the picture of a **balance scale** that shows plums lighter than bananas?

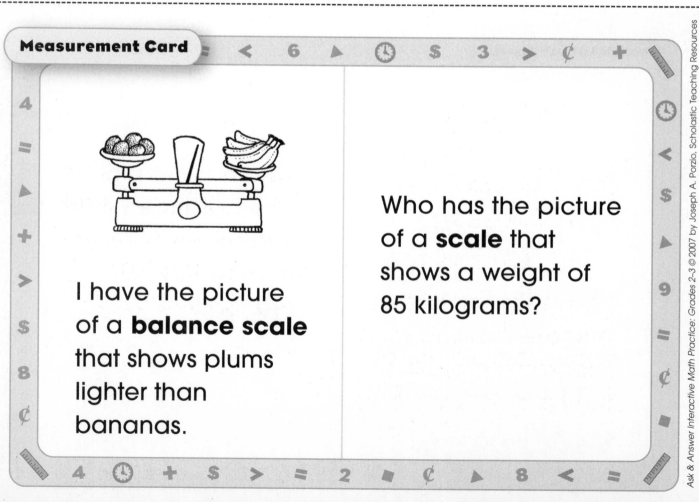

I have the picture of a **balance scale** that shows plums lighter than bananas.

Who has the picture of a **scale** that shows a weight of 85 kilograms?

Ask & Answer Interactive Math Practice: Grades 2–3 © 2007 by Joseph A. Porzio, Scholastic Teaching Resources

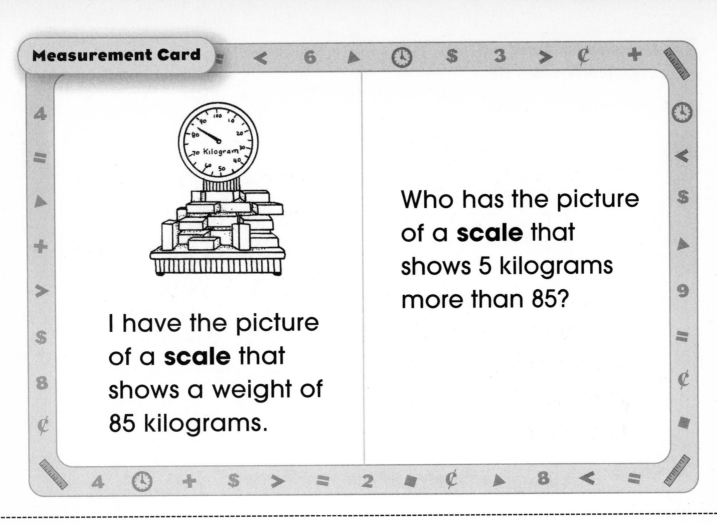

I have the picture of a **scale** that shows a weight of 85 kilograms.

Who has the picture of a **scale** that shows 5 kilograms more than 85?

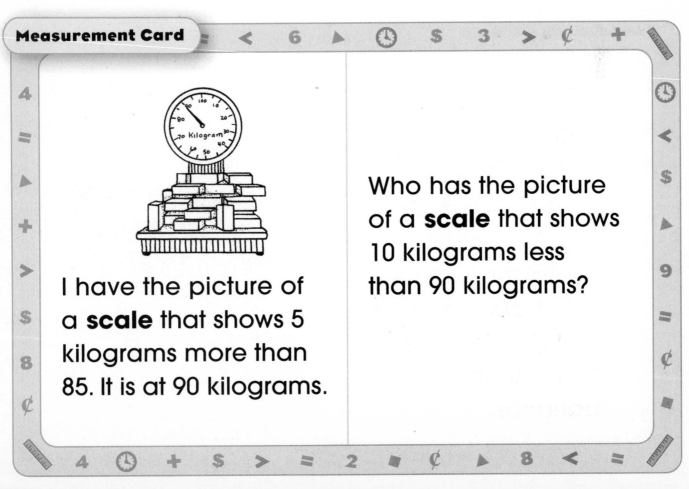

I have the picture of a **scale** that shows 5 kilograms more than 85. It is at 90 kilograms.

Who has the picture of a **scale** that shows 10 kilograms less than 90 kilograms?

Ask & Answer Interactive Math Practice: Grades 2–3 © 2007 by Joseph A. Porzio, Scholastic Teaching Resources

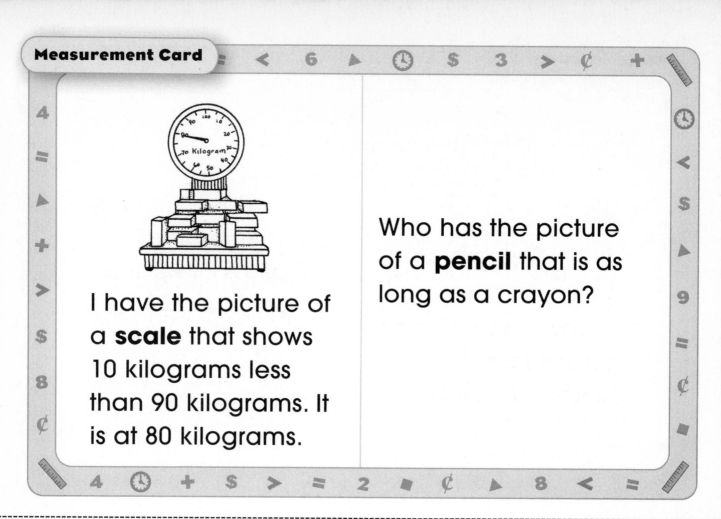

I have the picture of a **scale** that shows 10 kilograms less than 90 kilograms. It is at 80 kilograms.

Who has the picture of a **pencil** that is as long as a crayon?

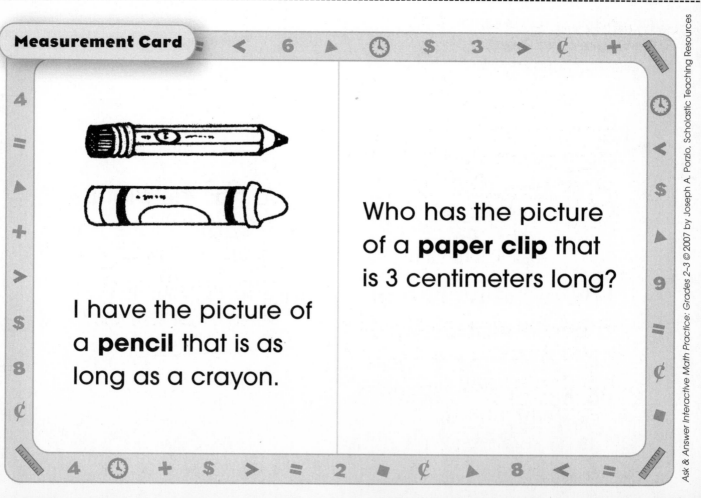

I have the picture of a **pencil** that is as long as a crayon.

Who has the picture of a **paper clip** that is 3 centimeters long?

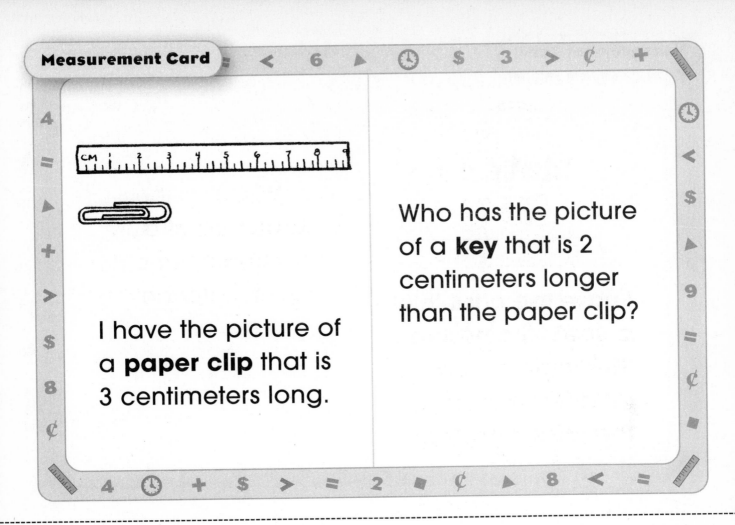

I have the picture of a **paper clip** that is 3 centimeters long.

Who has the picture of a **key** that is 2 centimeters longer than the paper clip?

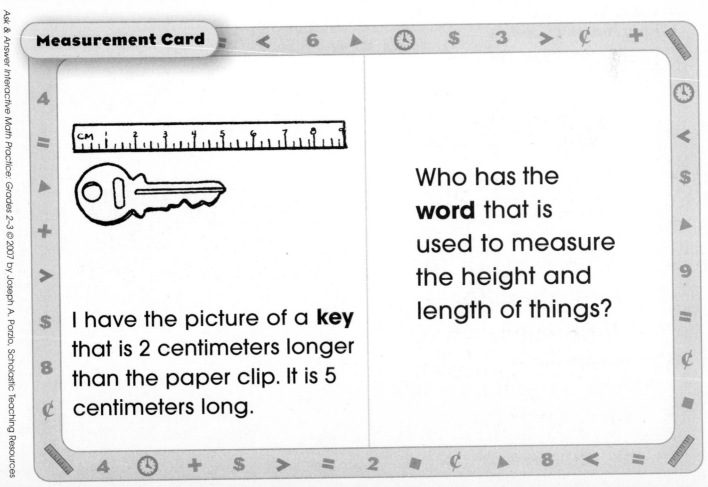

I have the picture of a **key** that is 2 centimeters longer than the paper clip. It is 5 centimeters long.

Who has the **word** that is used to measure the height and length of things?

meter

I have the **word** that is used to measure the height and length of things. The word is *meter*.

Who has the picture of a **student** who is taller than a meter?

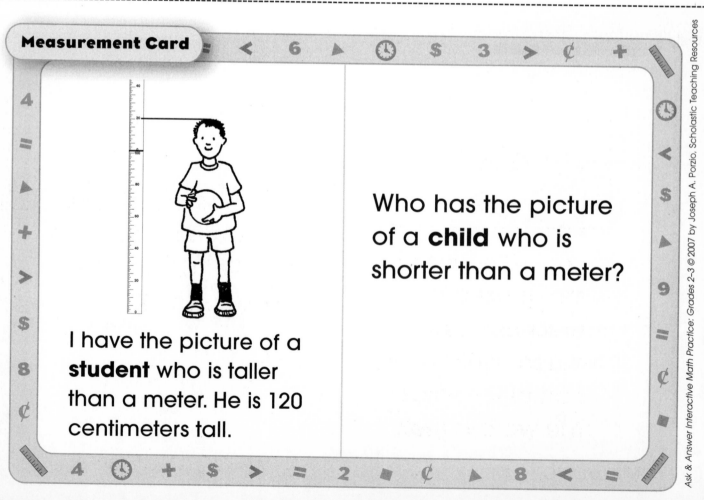

I have the picture of a **student** who is taller than a meter. He is 120 centimeters tall.

Who has the picture of a **child** who is shorter than a meter?

Ask & Answer Interactive Math Practice: Grades 2–3 © 2007 by Joseph A. Porzio, Scholastic Teaching Resources

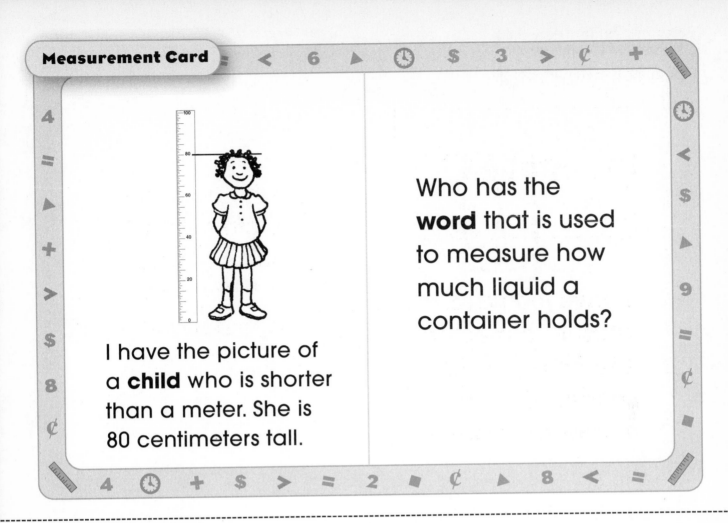

I have the picture of a **child** who is shorter than a meter. She is 80 centimeters tall.

Who has the **word** that is used to measure how much liquid a container holds?

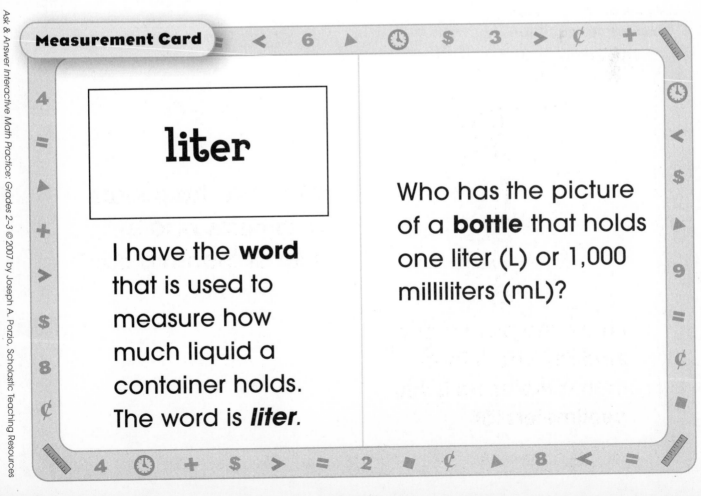

liter

I have the **word** that is used to measure how much liquid a container holds. The word is *liter*.

Who has the picture of a **bottle** that holds one liter (L) or 1,000 milliliters (mL)?

Ask & Answer Interactive Math Practice: Grades 2-3 © 2007 by Joseph A. Porzio, Scholastic Teaching Resources

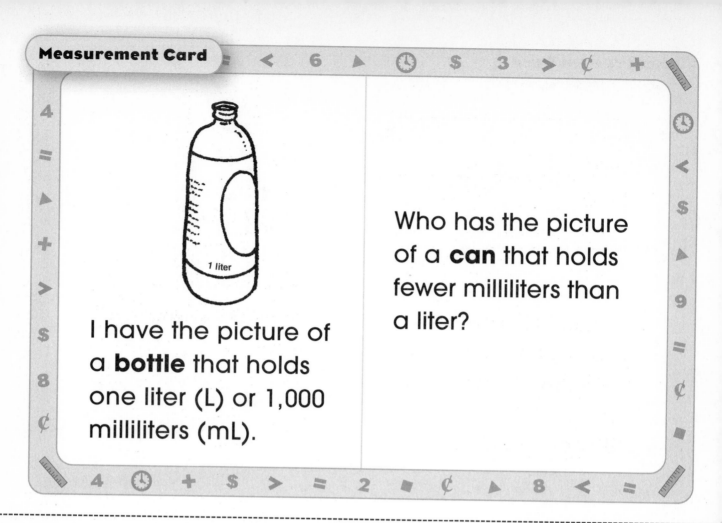

I have the picture of a **bottle** that holds one liter (L) or 1,000 milliliters (mL).

Who has the picture of a **can** that holds fewer milliliters than a liter?

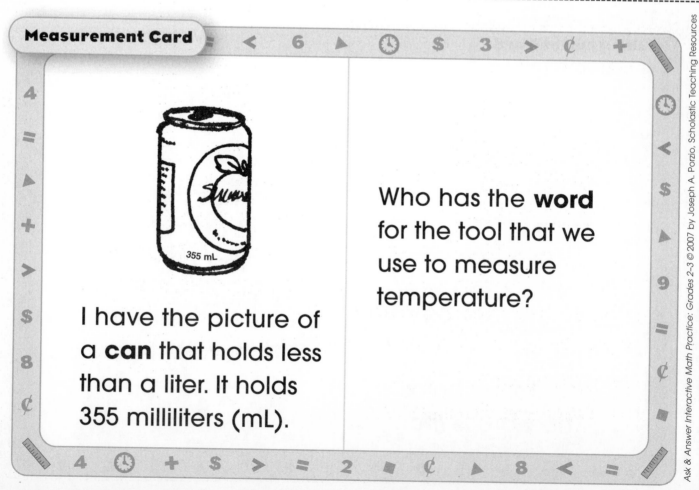

I have the picture of a **can** that holds less than a liter. It holds 355 milliliters (mL).

Who has the **word** for the tool that we use to measure temperature?

Ask & Answer Interactive Math Practice: Grades 2–3 © 2007 by Joseph A. Porzio. Scholastic Teaching Resources

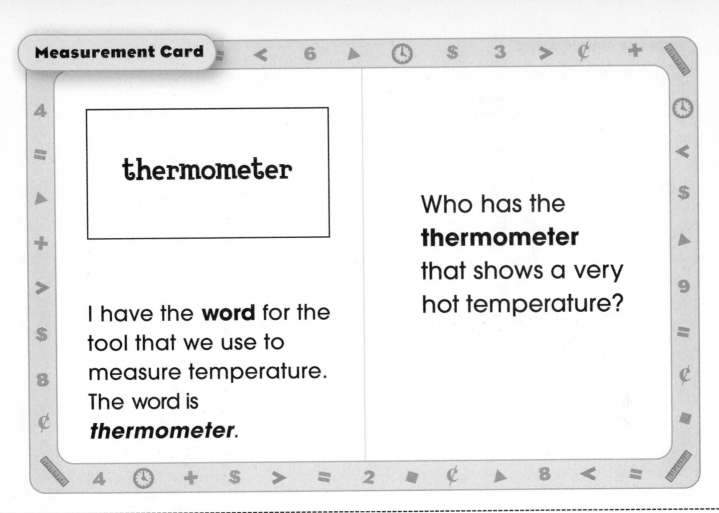

thermometer

I have the **word** for the tool that we use to measure temperature. The word is *thermometer*.

Who has the **thermometer** that shows a very hot temperature?

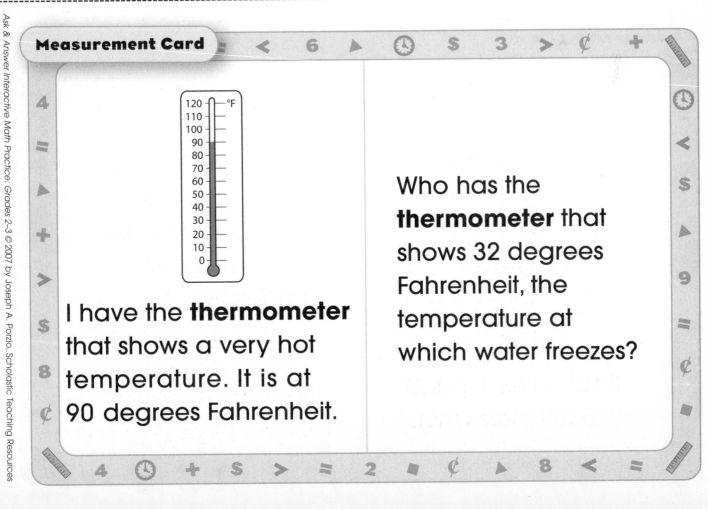

I have the **thermometer** that shows a very hot temperature. It is at 90 degrees Fahrenheit.

Who has the **thermometer** that shows 32 degrees Fahrenheit, the temperature at which water freezes?

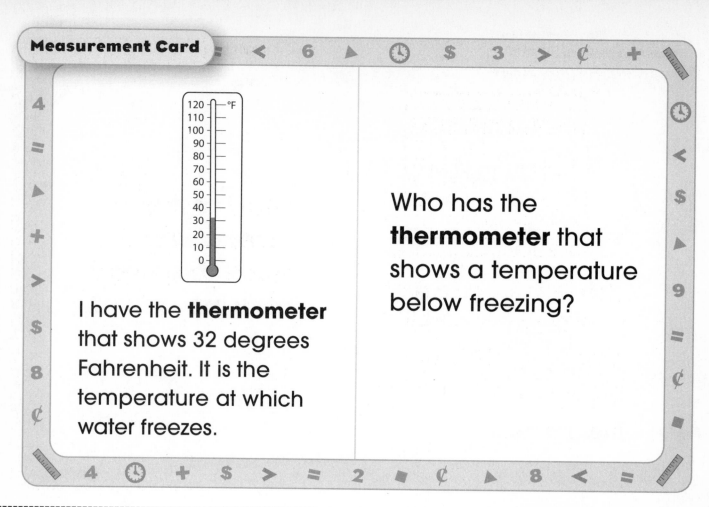

Measurement Card

I have the **thermometer** that shows 32 degrees Fahrenheit. It is the temperature at which water freezes.

Who has the **thermometer** that shows a temperature below freezing?

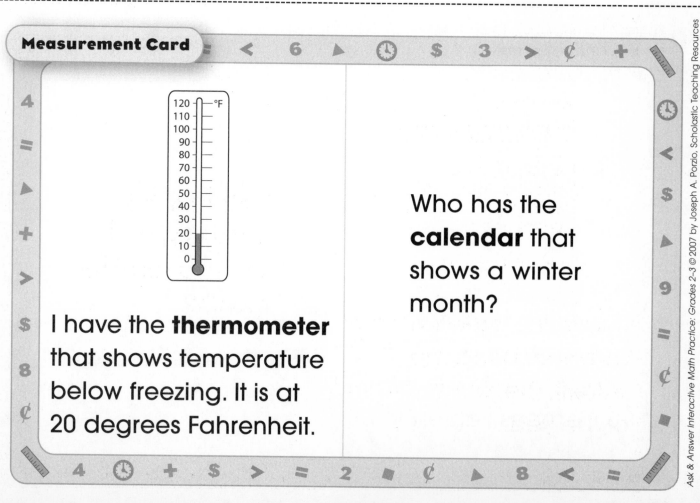

Measurement Card

I have the **thermometer** that shows temperature below freezing. It is at 20 degrees Fahrenheit.

Who has the **calendar** that shows a winter month?

Ask & Answer Interactive Math Practice: Grades 2–3 © 2007 by Joseph A. Porzio, Scholastic Teaching Resources

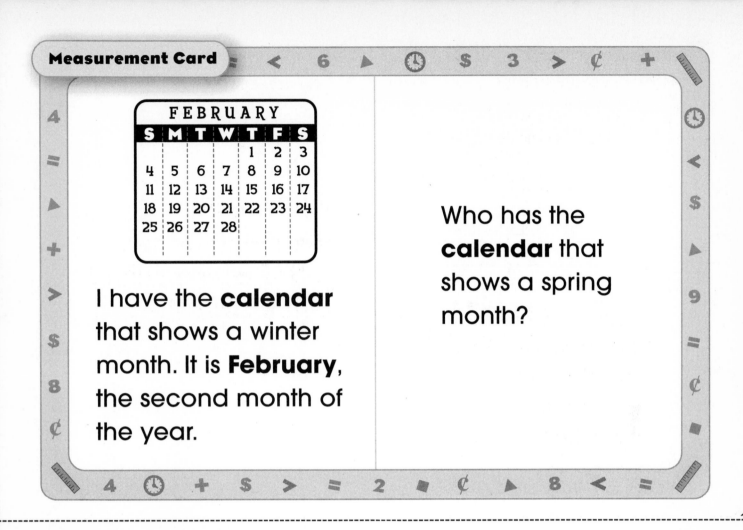

I have the **calendar** that shows a winter month. It is **February**, the second month of the year.

Who has the **calendar** that shows a spring month?

Ask & Answer Interactive Math Practice: Grades 2–3 © 2007 by Joseph A. Porzio, Scholastic Teaching Resources

I have the **calendar** that shows a spring month. It is April, the fourth month of the year.

Who has the **calendar** that shows a summer month?

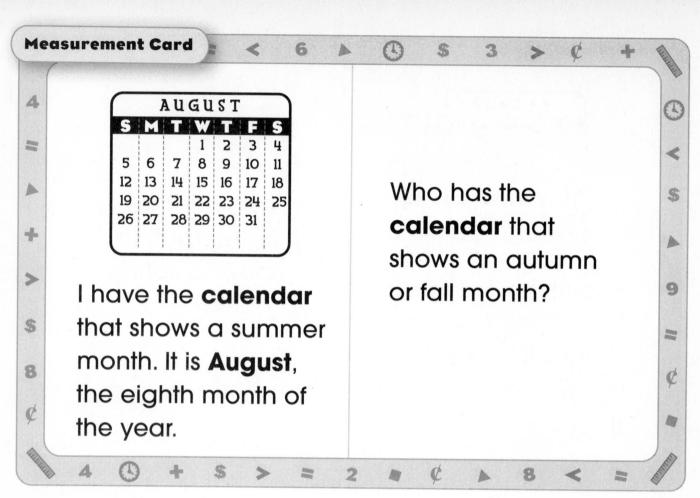

I have the **calendar** that shows a summer month. It is **August**, the eighth month of the year.

Who has the **calendar** that shows an autumn or fall month?

I have the **calendar** that shows an autumn or fall month. It is **October**, the tenth month of the year.

And that's the long and short of **measurement**!

Geometry is all about shapes. Let's start with a simple one.

Who has the picture of a **circle**?

Ask & Answer Interactive Math Practice: Grades 2–3 © 2007 by Joseph A. Porzio, Scholastic Teaching Resources

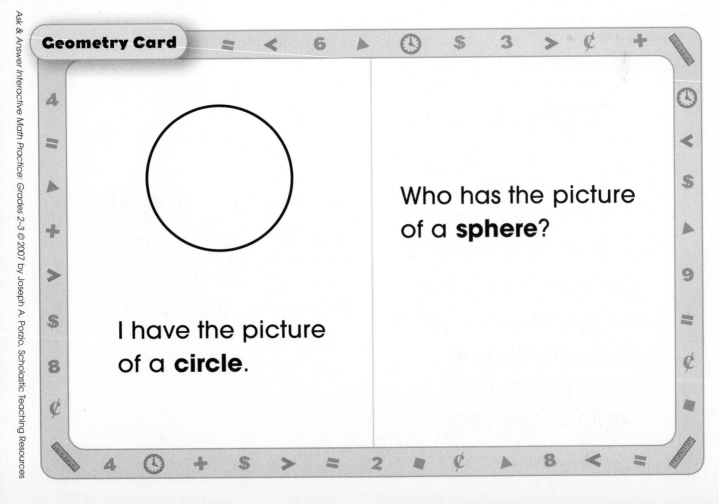

Who has the picture of a **sphere**?

I have the picture of a **circle**.

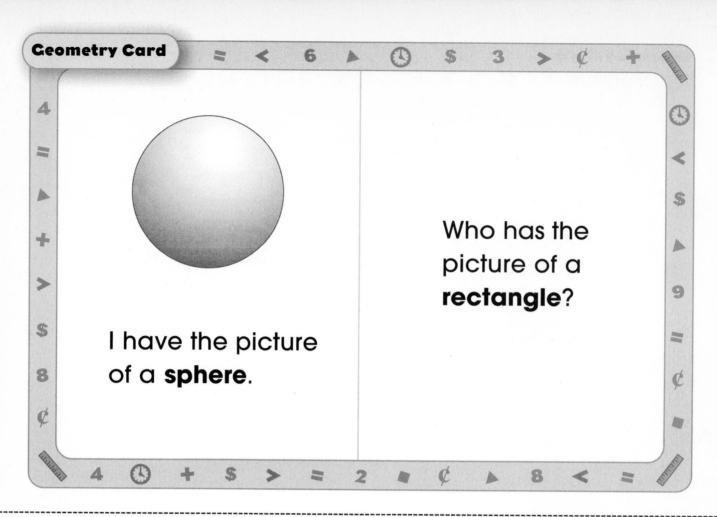

I have the picture of a **sphere**.

Who has the picture of a **rectangle**?

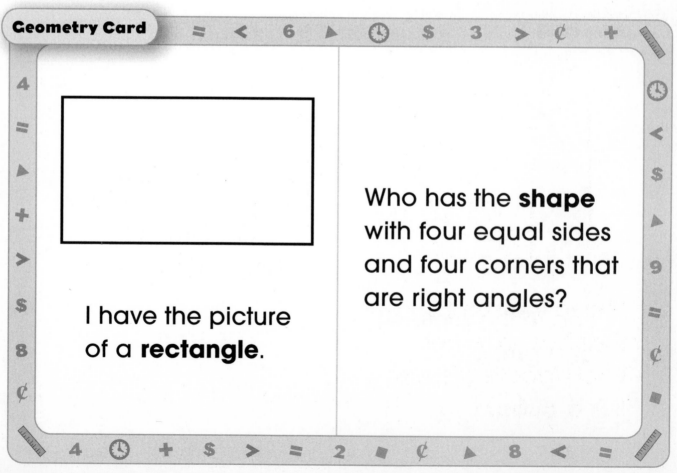

I have the picture of a **rectangle**.

Who has the **shape** with four equal sides and four corners that are right angles?

Ask & Answer Interactive Math Practice: Grades 2–3 © 2007 by Joseph A. Porzio, Scholastic Teaching Resources

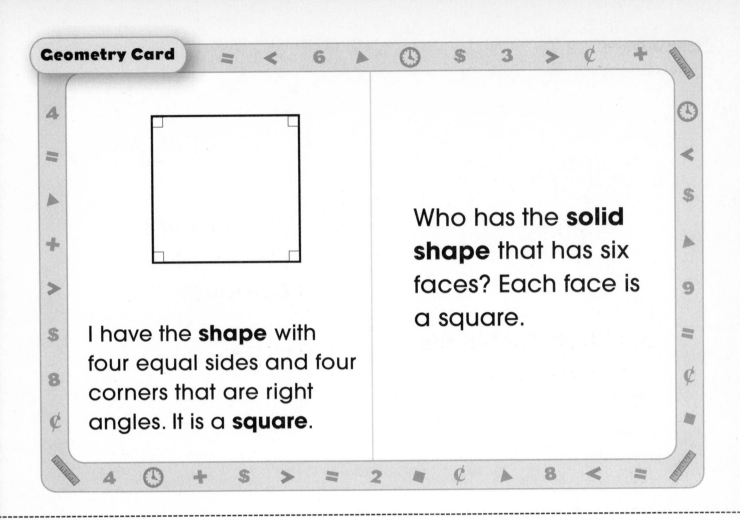

I have the **shape** with four equal sides and four corners that are right angles. It is a **square**.

Who has the **solid shape** that has six faces? Each face is a square.

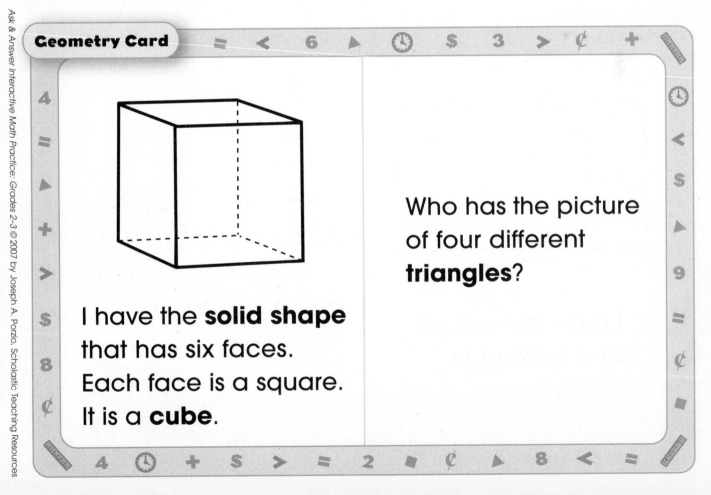

I have the **solid shape** that has six faces. Each face is a square. It is a **cube**.

Who has the picture of four different **triangles**?

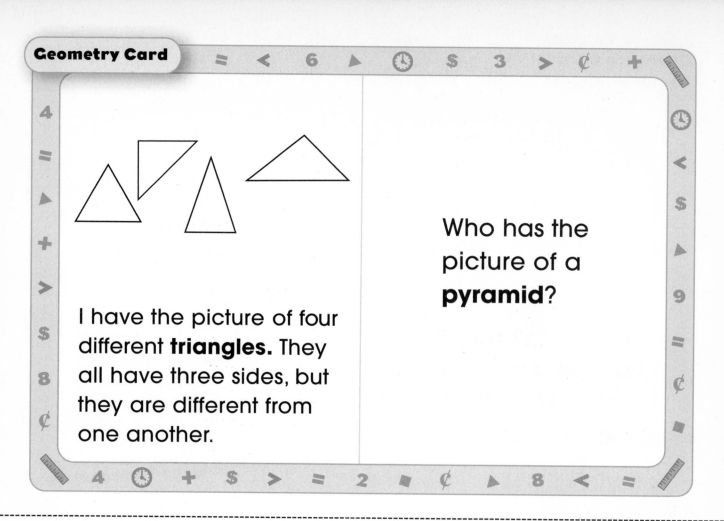

I have the picture of four different **triangles.** They all have three sides, but they are different from one another.

Who has the picture of a **pyramid**?

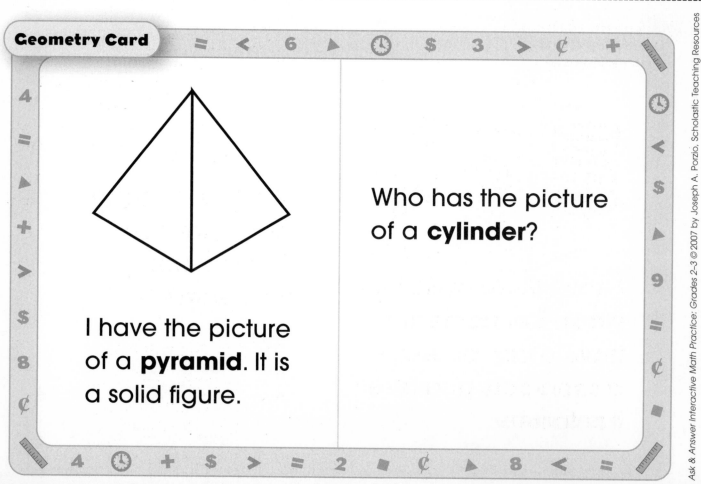

Who has the picture of a **cylinder**?

I have the picture of a **pyramid**. It is a solid figure.

Ask & Answer Interactive Math Practice: Grades 2–3 © 2007 by Joseph A. Porzio, Scholastic Teaching Resources

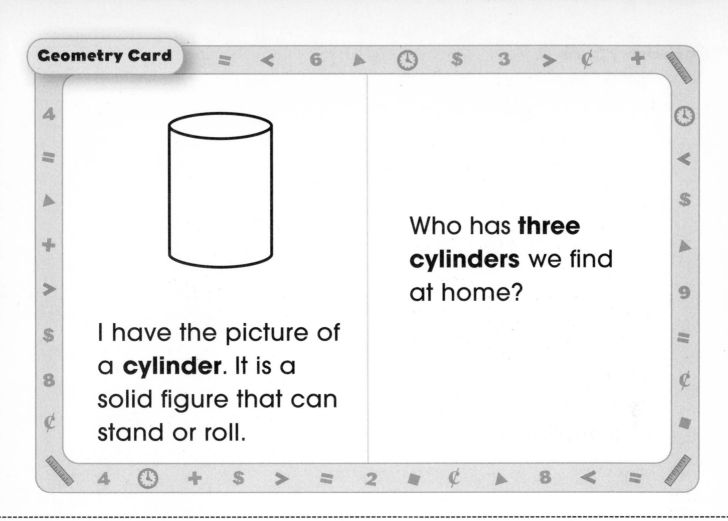

I have the picture of a **cylinder**. It is a solid figure that can stand or roll.

Who has **three cylinders** we find at home?

Ask & Answer Interactive Math Practice: Grades 2–3 © 2007 by Joseph A. Porzio, Scholastic Teaching Resources

Geometry Card

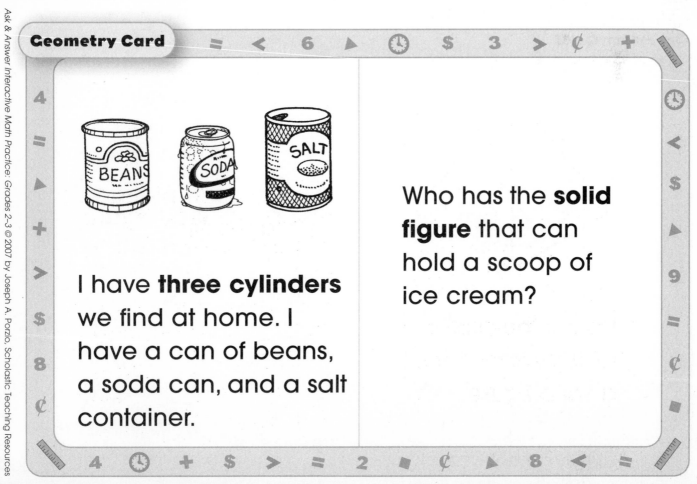

I have **three cylinders** we find at home. I have a can of beans, a soda can, and a salt container.

Who has the **solid figure** that can hold a scoop of ice cream?

= < 6 ▶ 🕐 $ 3 > ¢ +

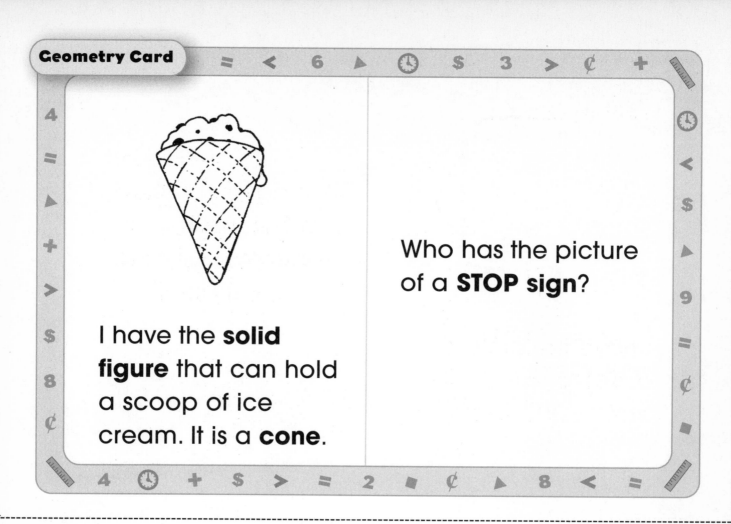

I have the **solid figure** that can hold a scoop of ice cream. It is a **cone**.

Who has the picture of a **STOP sign**?

4 🕐 + $ > = 2 ■ ¢ ▶ 8 < =

= < 6 ▶ 🕐 $ 3 > ¢ +

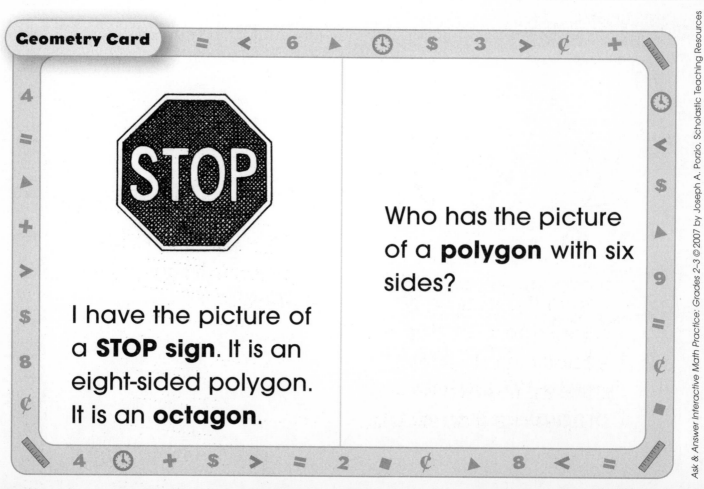

I have the picture of a **STOP sign**. It is an eight-sided polygon. It is an **octagon**.

Who has the picture of a **polygon** with six sides?

4 🕐 + $ > = 2 ■ ¢ ▶ 8 < =

Ask & Answer Interactive Math Practice: Grades 2–3 © 2007 by Joseph A. Porzio, Scholastic Teaching Resources

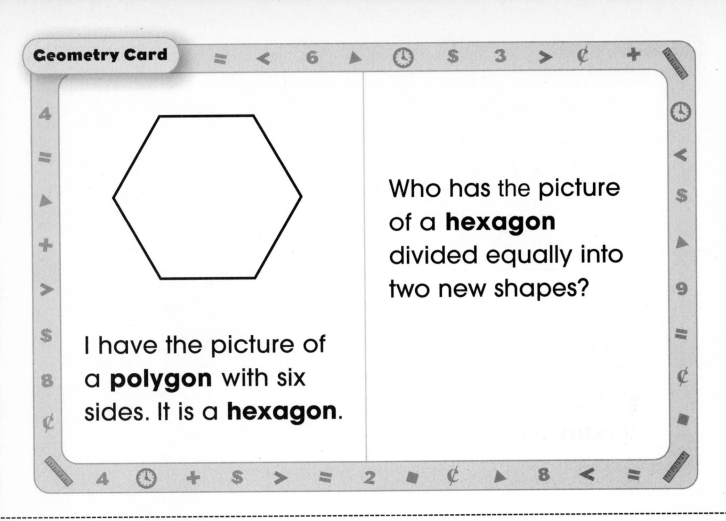

Who has the picture of a **hexagon** divided equally into two new shapes?

I have the picture of a **polygon** with six sides. It is a **hexagon**.

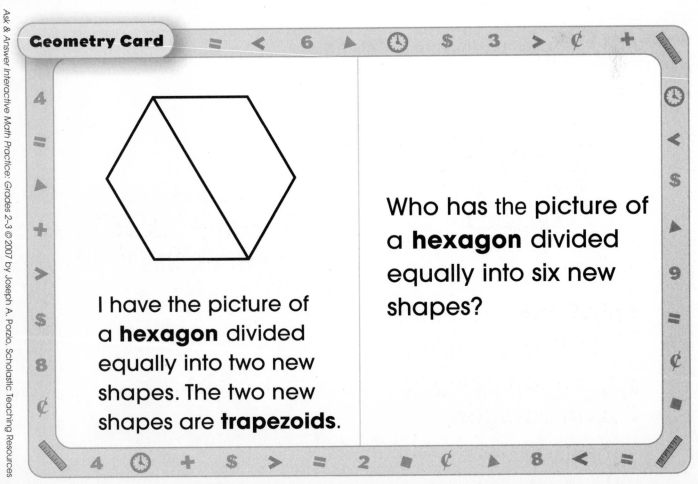

Who has the picture of a **hexagon** divided equally into six new shapes?

I have the picture of a **hexagon** divided equally into two new shapes. The two new shapes are **trapezoids**.

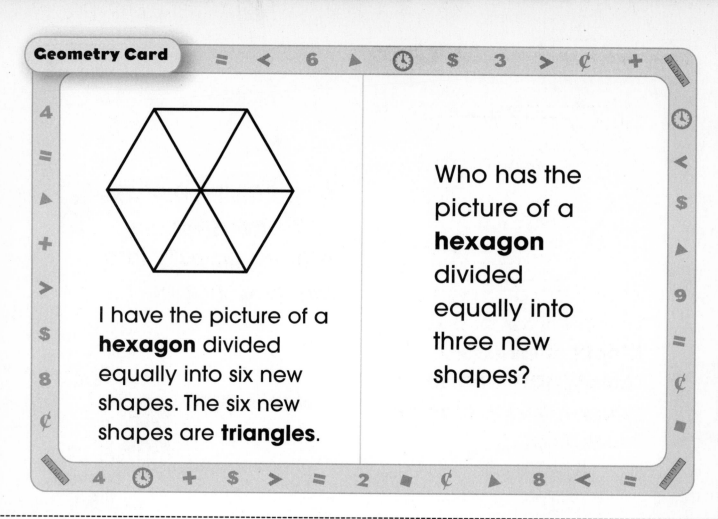

I have the picture of a **hexagon** divided equally into six new shapes. The six new shapes are **triangles**.

Who has the picture of a **hexagon** divided equally into three new shapes?

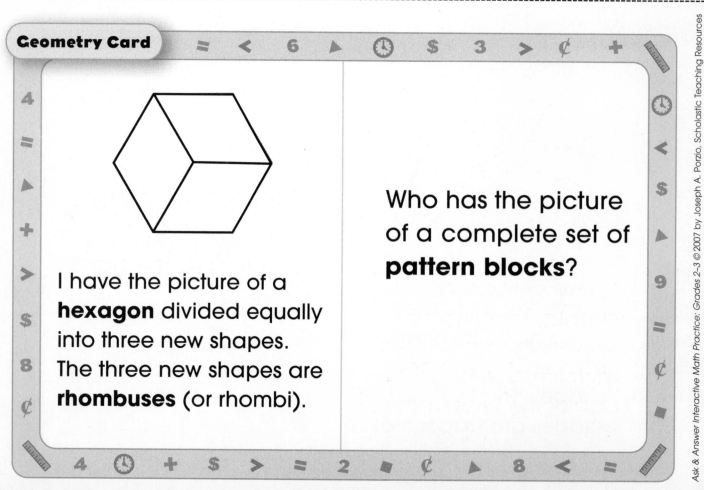

I have the picture of a **hexagon** divided equally into three new shapes. The three new shapes are **rhombuses** (or rhombi).

Who has the picture of a complete set of **pattern blocks**?

Ask & Answer Interactive Math Practice: Grades 2–3 © 2007 by Joseph A. Porzio, Scholastic Teaching Resources

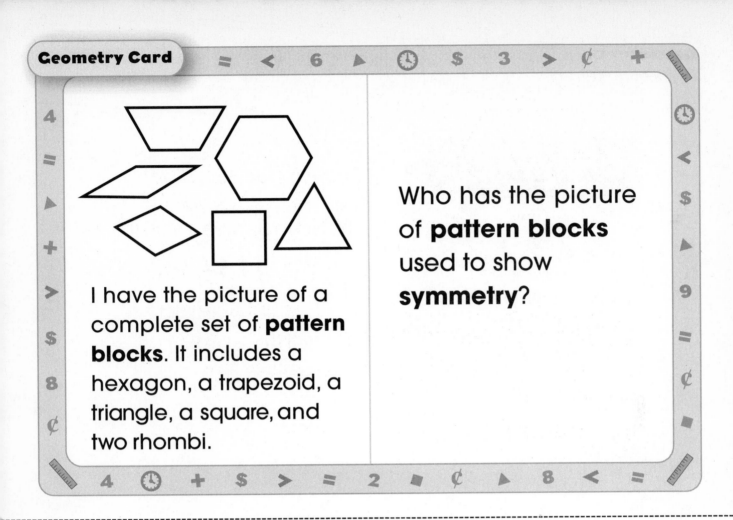

I have the picture of a complete set of **pattern blocks**. It includes a hexagon, a trapezoid, a triangle, a square, and two rhombi.

Who has the picture of **pattern blocks** used to show **symmetry**?

Geometry Card

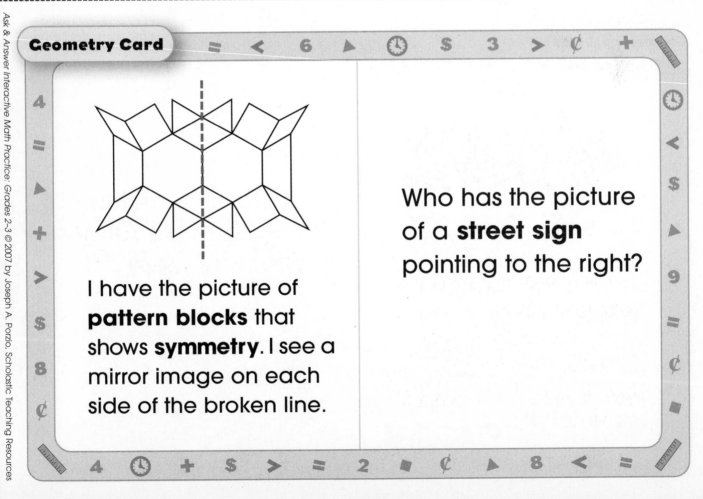

I have the picture of **pattern blocks** that shows **symmetry**. I see a mirror image on each side of the broken line.

Who has the picture of a **street sign** pointing to the right?

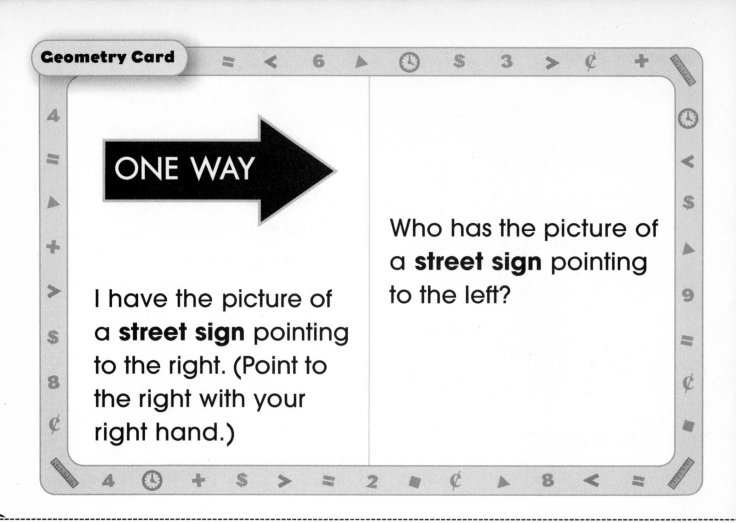

I have the picture of a **street sign** pointing to the right. (Point to the right with your right hand.)

Who has the picture of a **street sign** pointing to the left?

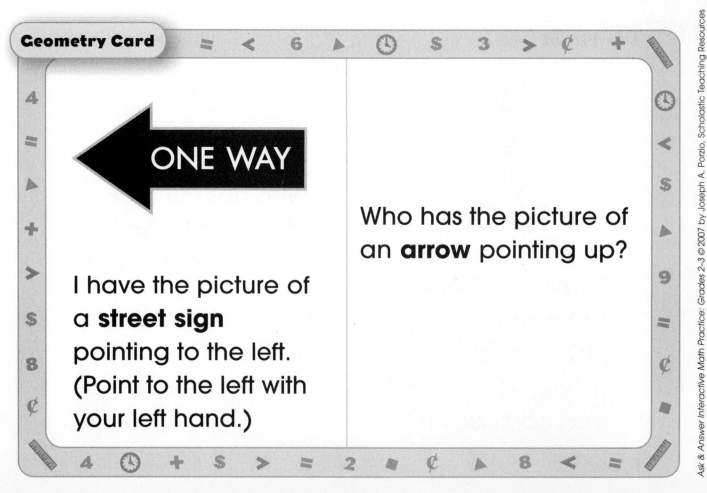

I have the picture of a **street sign** pointing to the left. (Point to the left with your left hand.)

Who has the picture of an **arrow** pointing up?

Ask & Answer Interactive Math Practice: Grades 2–3 © 2007 by Joseph A. Porzio, Scholastic Teaching Resources

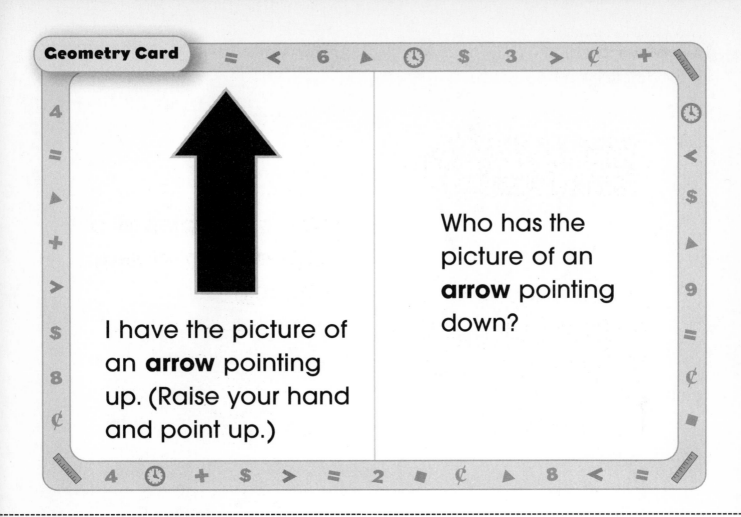

I have the picture of an **arrow** pointing up. (Raise your hand and point up.)

Who has the picture of an **arrow** pointing down?

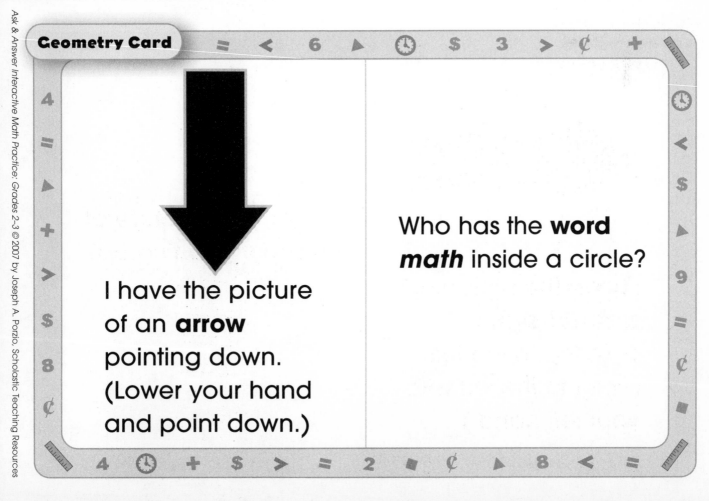

I have the picture of an **arrow** pointing down. (Lower your hand and point down.)

Who has the **word** *math* inside a circle?

Ask & Answer Interactive Math Practice: Grades 2–3 © 2007 by Joseph A. Porzio, Scholastic Teaching Resources

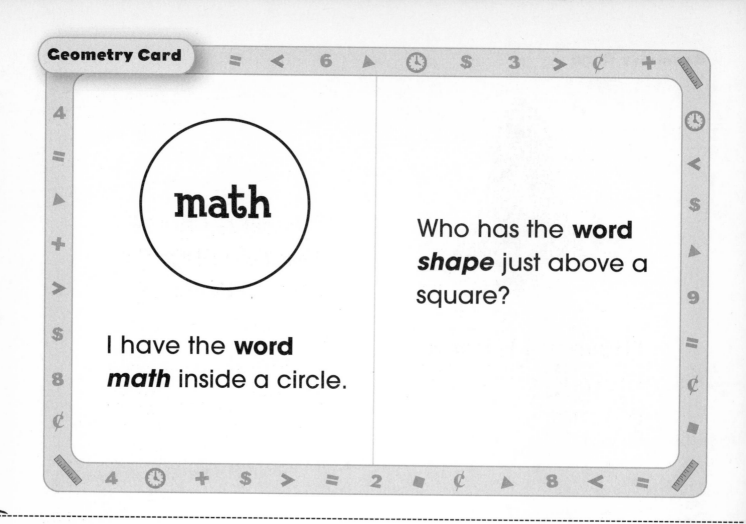

math

I have the **word math** inside a circle.

Who has the **word shape** just above a square?

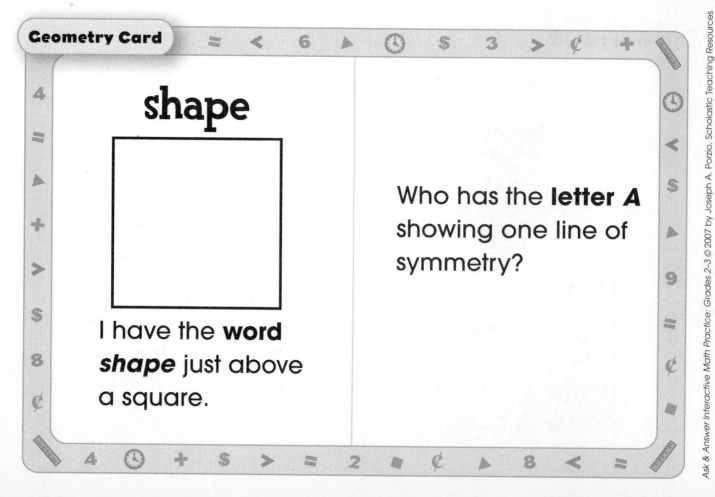

shape

I have the **word shape** just above a square.

Who has the **letter A** showing one line of symmetry?

Ask & Answer Interactive Math Practice: Grades 2–3 © 2007 by Joseph A. Porzio, Scholastic Teaching Resources

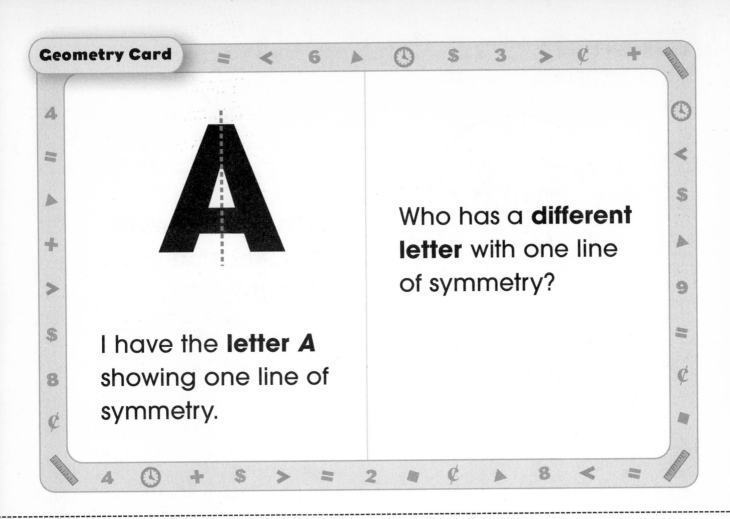

I have the **letter A** showing one line of symmetry.

Who has a **different letter** with one line of symmetry?

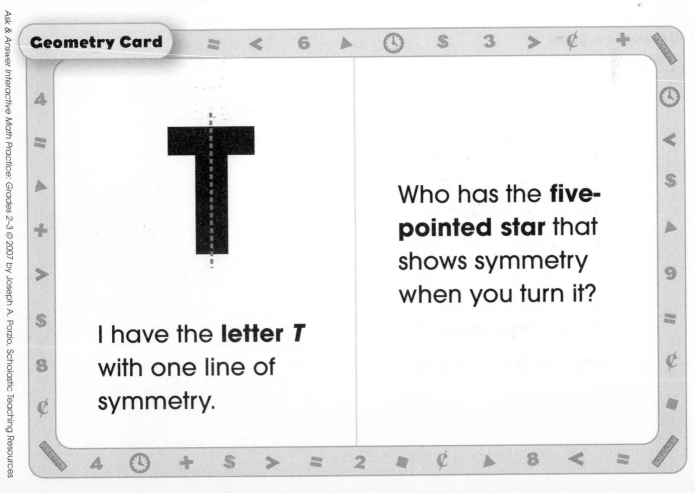

I have the **letter T** with one line of symmetry.

Who has the **five-pointed star** that shows symmetry when you turn it?

Ask & Answer Interactive Math Practice: Grades 2–3 © 2007 by Joseph A. Porzio. Scholastic Teaching Resources

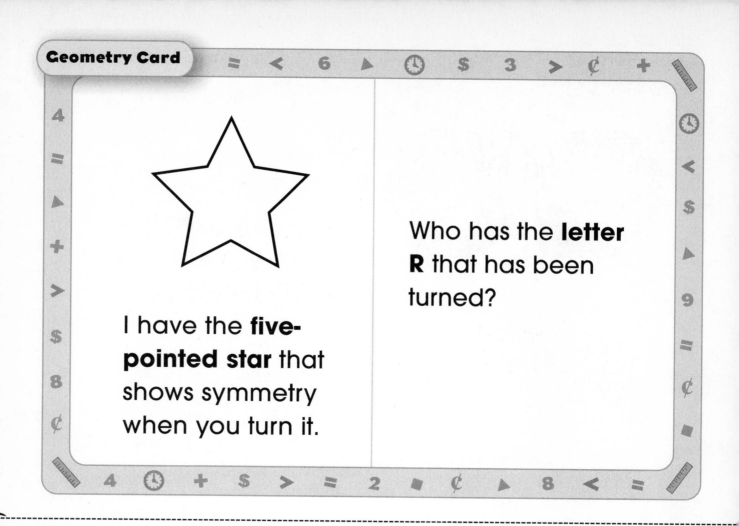

I have the **five-pointed star** that shows symmetry when you turn it.

Who has the **letter R** that has been turned?

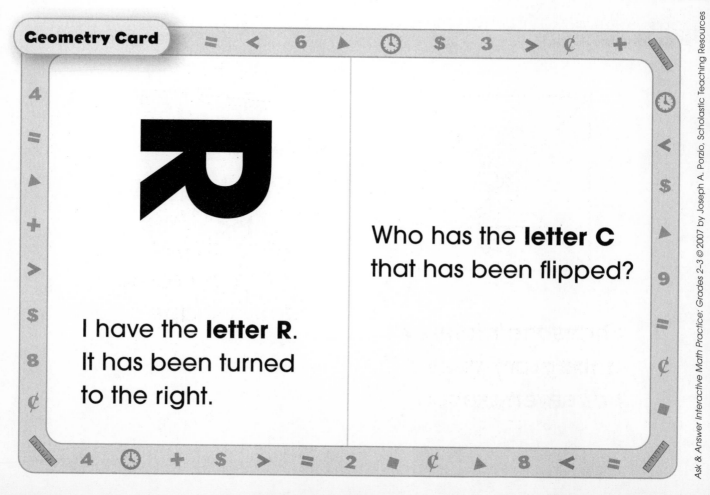

I have the **letter R**. It has been turned to the right.

Who has the **letter C** that has been flipped?

Ask & Answer Interactive Math Practice: Grades 2–3 © 2007 by Joseph A. Porzio, Scholastic Teaching Resources

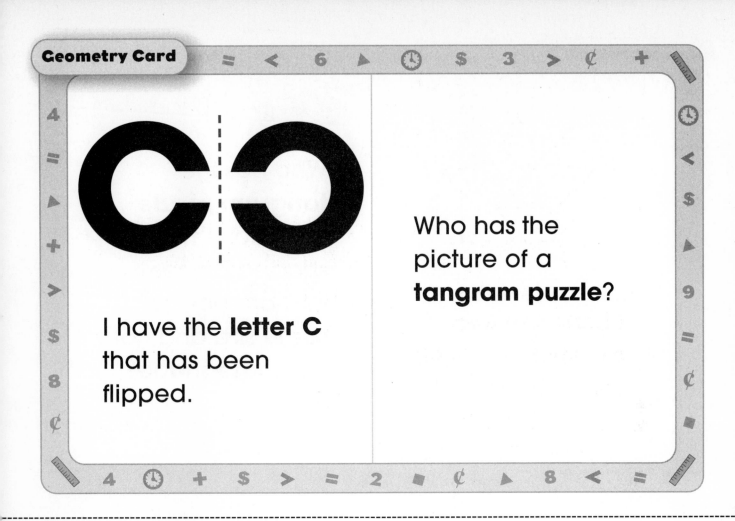

I have the **letter C** that has been flipped.

Who has the picture of a **tangram puzzle**?

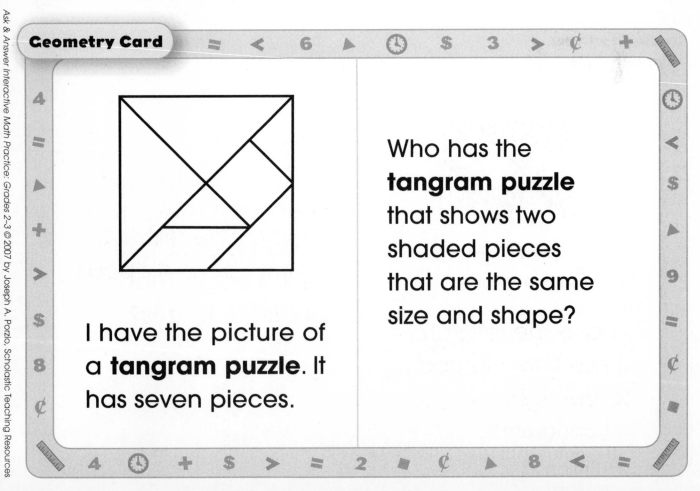

I have the picture of a **tangram puzzle**. It has seven pieces.

Who has the **tangram puzzle** that shows two shaded pieces that are the same size and shape?

I have the **tangram puzzle** that shows two shaded pieces that are the same size and shape. The two shaded pieces are **congruent**.

Who has the **tangram puzzle** that shows two shaded pieces that are not the same size and not the same shape?

I have the **tangram puzzle** that shows two shaded pieces that are not the same size and not the same shape. The two shaded pieces are not congruent.

Who has the **tangram puzzle** that shows two shaded pieces that are the same shape but different sizes?

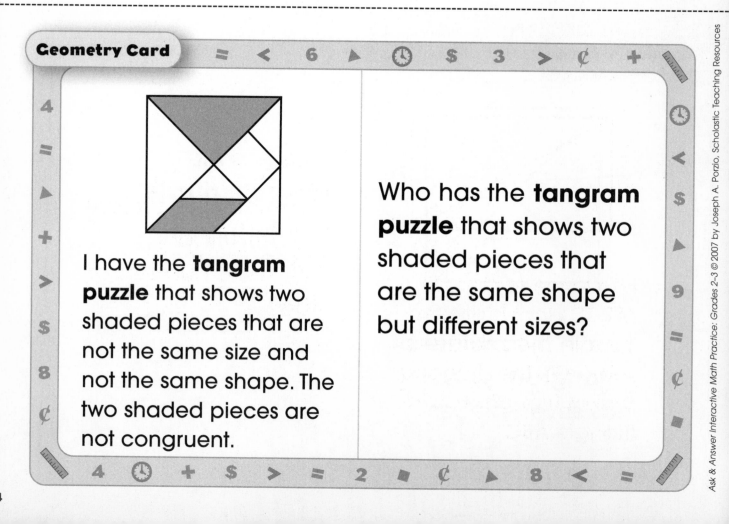

Ask & Answer Interactive Math Practice: Grades 2–3 © 2007 by Joseph A. Porzio, Scholastic Teaching Resources

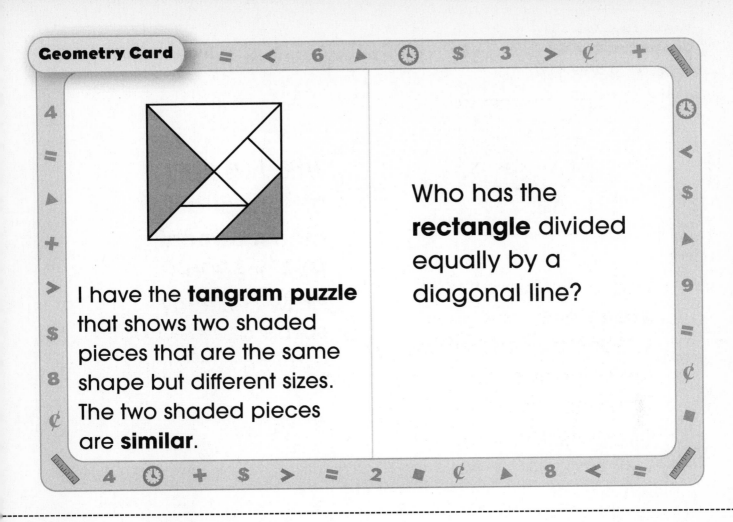

I have the **tangram puzzle** that shows two shaded pieces that are the same shape but different sizes. The two shaded pieces are **similar**.

Who has the **rectangle** divided equally by a diagonal line?

Ask & Answer Interactive Math Practice: Grades 2–3 © 2007 by Joseph A. Porzio, Scholastic Teaching Resources

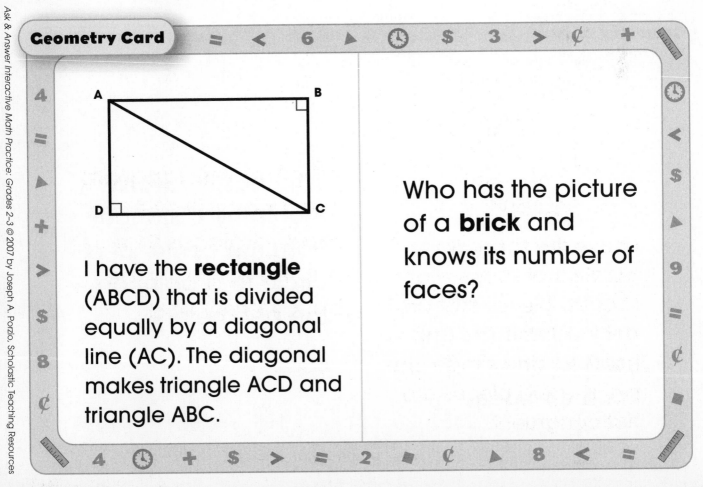

I have the **rectangle** (ABCD) that is divided equally by a diagonal line (AC). The diagonal makes triangle ACD and triangle ABC.

Who has the picture of a **brick** and knows its number of faces?

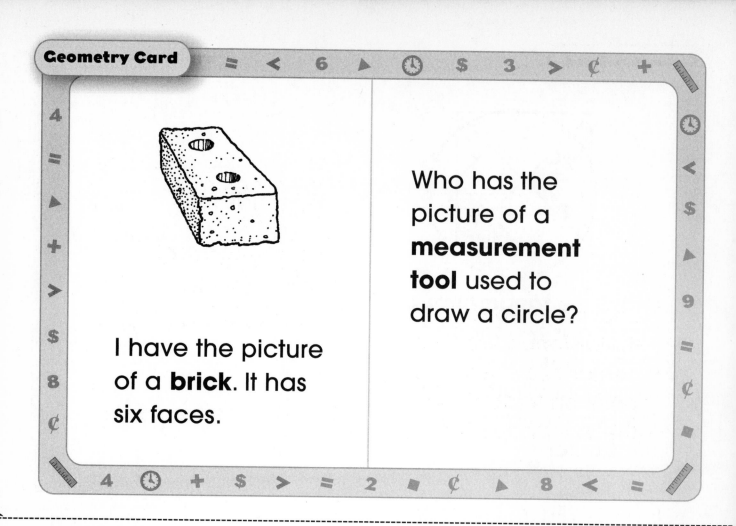

I have the picture of a **brick**. It has six faces.

Who has the picture of a **measurement tool** used to draw a circle?

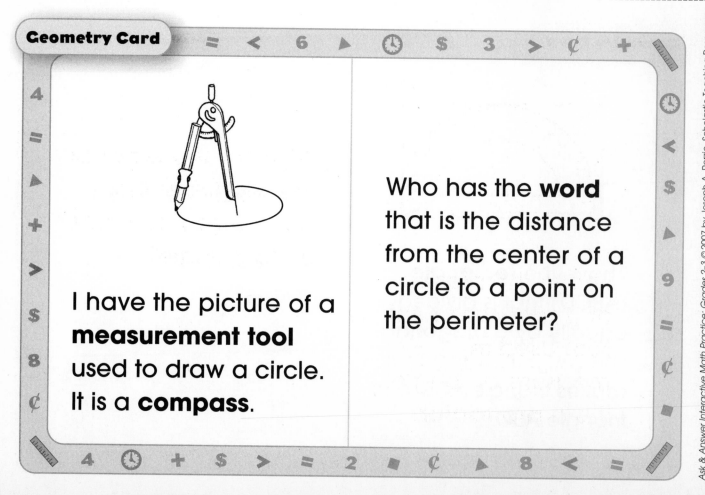

I have the picture of a **measurement tool** used to draw a circle. It is a **compass**.

Who has the **word** that is the distance from the center of a circle to a point on the perimeter?

Ask & Answer Interactive Math Practice: Grades 2–3 © 2007 by Joseph A. Porzio, Scholastic Teaching Resources

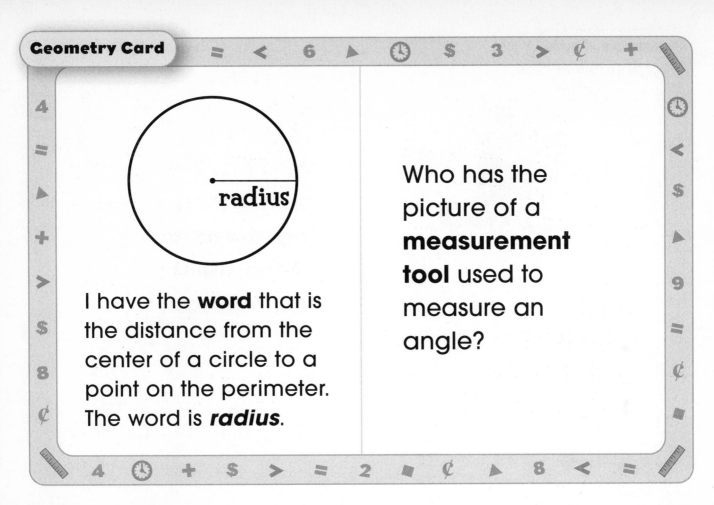

I have the **word** that is the distance from the center of a circle to a point on the perimeter. The word is *radius*.

Who has the picture of a **measurement tool** used to measure an angle?

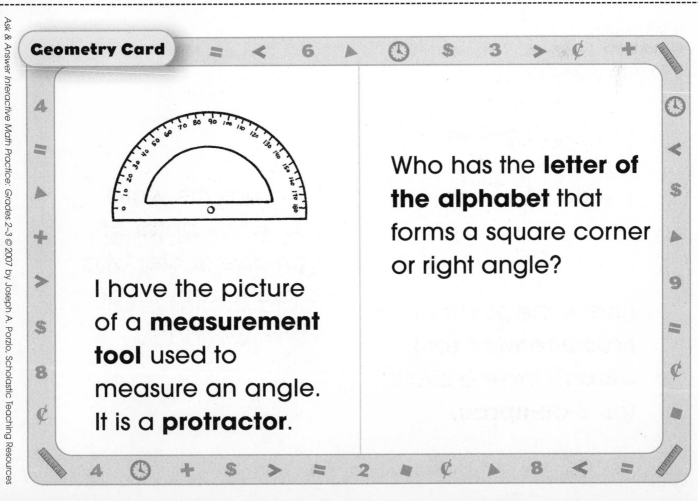

I have the picture of a **measurement tool** used to measure an angle. It is a **protractor**.

Who has the **letter of the alphabet** that forms a square corner or right angle?

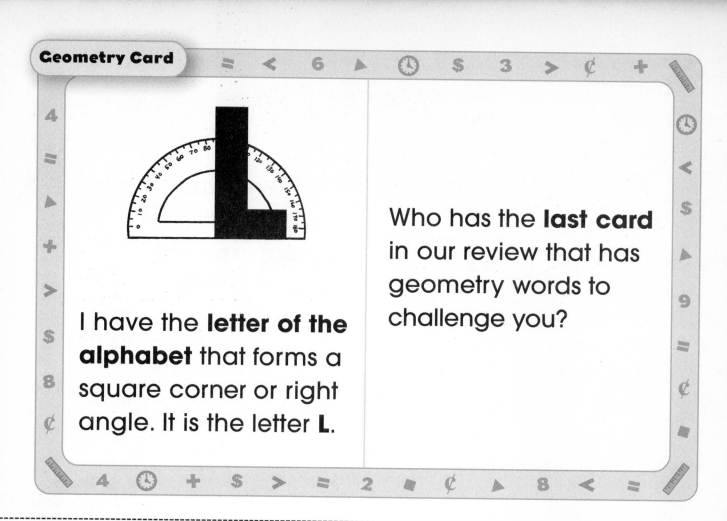

I have the **letter of the alphabet** that forms a square corner or right angle. It is the letter **L**.

Who has the **last card** in our review that has geometry words to challenge you?

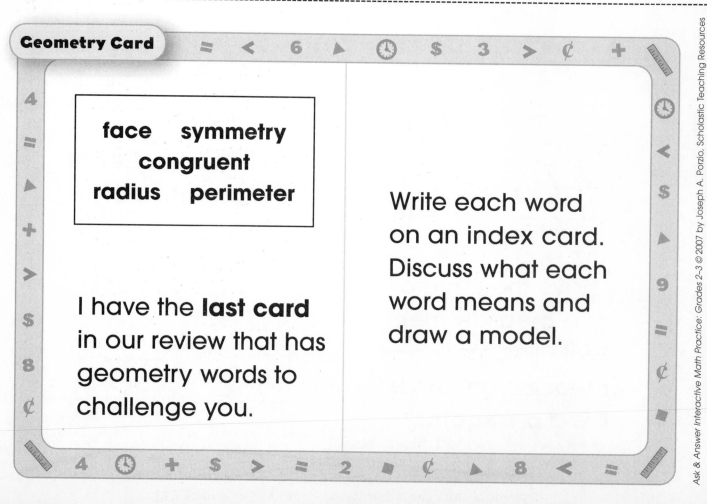

face   symmetry
congruent
radius   perimeter

I have the **last card** in our review that has geometry words to challenge you.

Write each word on an index card. Discuss what each word means and draw a model.

Ask & Answer Interactive Math Practice: Grades 2–3 © 2007 by Joseph A. Porzio, Scholastic Teaching Resources